Preface

Planning is absolutely key if you hope to deliver inspiring lessons that both motivate and engage your students. A lesson plan is the instructor's road map of what students need to learn and how it will be done effectively during the class time.

Effective lesson planning is essential to the process of teaching and learning. Before you plan your lesson, you will first need to identify the learning objectives for the class meeting. Effective lesson preparation to ensure student learning is part of a cyclical process of planning, doing and evaluations link 'backwards' and forwards' throughout the planning process.

A successful lesson plan addresses and integrates these three key components:
- Objectives for student learning
- Teaching/learning activities
- Strategies to check student understanding

Specifying concrete objectives for student learning will help you to determine the kinds of teaching and learning activities you will use in class, while those activities will define how you will check whether the learning objectives have been accomplished.

The aim of this book is to help you, as a teacher, to further understand the principles of effective lesson planning. This will involve developing your knowledge of what promotes student learning,

In this book, best and interesting lesson plans are prepared which will be helpful to develop a different type of confidence in pupil-teacher.

I wish you a successful and rewarding career.

– Manmeet Kaur

Acknowledgement

My compliments go to the **GullyBaba Publishing House (P) Ltd.,** and its meticulous team who have been enthusiastically working towards the perfection of the book.

Their teamwork, initiative and research have been very encouraging. Had it not been for their unflagging support, this work wouldn't have been possible. The creative freedom provided by them along with their aim of presenting the best to the reader has been a major source of inspiration in this work. Hope that this book would be successful.

– Manmeet Kaur

Publisher's Note

The lesson plan "English" is prepared to apprise student on the formulation of the same. With the advent of technology and the Internet, there has been no dearth of information available to all; however, finding the relevant and qualitative information, which is focused, is an uphill task.

We at **GullyBaba Publishing House (P) Ltd.,** have taken this step to provide quality material which can accentuate in-depth knowledge about the subject. GPH books are a pioneer in the effort of providing unique and quality material to its readers. With our books, you are sure to attain success by making use of this powerful study material.

Our site **www.gullybaba.com** is a vital resource for your examination. The publisher wishes to acknowledge the significant contribution of the Team Members and our experts in bringing out this publication and highly thankful to Almighty God, without His blessings, this endeavor wouldn't have been successful.

– Publisher

Topics Covered

Composition
- Leave Application
- Essay Writing

Translation
- Present Perfect Tense
- Past Continuous Tense

4	Micro Teaching

5	Lesson Planning based on Microteaching

- Use of Articles
- Infinitive
- Participle
- Gerund

Contents

1 Introduction

●●●

Planning is usually interpreted as a process to develop a strategy to achieve desired objectives, to solve problems, and to facilitate action. It is equally true in relation to the teaching of any subject. Lesson plans will easily help one to achieve his/her goals and objectives, and same can be said on the part of his/her students or pupils.

A lesson plan is a teacher's detailed description of the course of instruction for an individual lesson. A daily lesson plan is developed by a teacher to guide class instruction. The detail of the plan will vary depending on the preference of the teacher, subject being covered, and the need and/or curiosity of children. There may be requirements mandated by the school system regarding the plan.

A well–developed lesson plan reflects the interests and needs of the students. It incorporates best practices for the educational field. The lesson plan correlates with the teacher's philosophy of education, which is what the teacher feels is the purpose of educating the students.

Meaning of Lesson Planning

A lesson plan outlines in detail the various steps which the teacher proposes to undertake in his/her class. As such, a lesson plan concerns itself with the teaching of one period. Planning for a lesson means identification of the sequence and style of presentation and evaluation procedure to be adopted for classroom teaching of a lesson. Hence, it is a proposition in advance which establishes a linkage between the why, what and how of teaching in one period. While attempting to do this, the teacher may foresee likely problems in classroom communication and may arrange certain materials and decide about techniques to be adopted to ensure a smooth and effective teaching–learning situation. Thus, a lesson plan is a means of taking advance decisions about the selection, sequencing and execution of various activities to be performed in a classroom with a view to ensuring learning of children.

Need and Importance of Lesson Planning

When a teacher goes for teaching a lesson in the classroom, usually s/he gets prepared for it though informally. But sometimes, s/he finds that s/he is not able to teach the entire content which s/he prepared or on the other hand, the content to be covered is not sufficient for full period. Sometime, s/he may get stuck–up while teaching and so get nervous. May be that s/he is not aware of the objectives of teaching a lesson and so did not bother about its attainment. How to overcome all such problems? This can be done through systematic lesson planning. S/he gets a chance of thinking about all these problems in advance while planning his/her lesson and deciding about taking corrective steps for possible hurdles. The process of developing a lesson plan is such that these problems get tackled automatically.

Lesson planning helps the teacher in the following ways:

- It makes teaching systematic and well organised.
- It helps teachers in identifying adequate content and its proper sequencing for teaching a lesson.
- It helps teachers to learn to foresee and tackle learning difficulties of children.
- It enables teachers to utilise the available time properly.

- It helps in developing insights about learning needs and abilities of children.
- It helps teachers to develop the habit of undertaking immediate corrective measures.
- It gives confidence to teachers during teaching.

By lesson planning, following abilities can be improved in students:

- Questioning
- Defining a Problem
- Hypothesising
- Planning a Solution
- Observing
- Discovering
- Discussing
- Recording
- Organising Knowledge
- Drawing Conclusions
- Generalising
- Understanding Relationship
- Using Previous Knowledge and Experience

Steps of Lesson Planning

While developing a lesson plan, first of all a teacher has to decide about the objectives of teaching that particular lesson. The objectives will be both general as well as specific. In order to achieve the objectives, some subject matter or content is required. This content is to be selected as per the competence with reference to the specific objectives of the lesson as well as the previous knowledge of the learner. So the content has to be local specific, interesting and related to the previous knowledge of the learner. Another important aspect of lesson planning is to detail out the method to be used for transacting the required material to the learners. The choice of method will depend on the nature of the content, the class/grade as well as the ability of the learners. While specifying the method of delivery, the teachers' activities as well as the learners' activities are to be specified along with the evaluation exercises/questions. The evaluation has to be based on the material transacted in the classroom and the competency aimed to be developed. At the primary stage, the evaluation questions have to be very simple, keeping in view the learners' physical and mental growth.

The following issues need to be decided for developing a lesson plan:

- **Objectives:** The objectives of teaching a particular lesson should be stated as per the competency to be developed amongst children. Generally, teachers state only general and specific objectives of the lesson.

- **Content:** The subject matter that is intended to be covered should be limited to the prescribed time. The matter must be interesting and it should be related to the pupils' previous knowledge. It should also be related to daily life situations.

- **Methods:** The most appropriate method be chosen by the teacher. The selected method, should be suitable to the subject matter to be taught. Suitable teaching aids must also be identified by the teacher. The teacher may also use supplementary aids to make his/her lesson more effective.

- **Evaluation:** A teacher must evaluate his/her lesson to find the extent to which s/he has achieved the objectives of his/her lesson. Evaluation can be done even by recapitulation of subject matter through suitable questions.

Various Forms of Lesson Planning

These are various forms of written lesson plans in our country and abroad, but following three forms are most popular and most commonly used:

(A) HERBARTIAN APPROACH TO LESSON PLANNING

The lesson planning is an ancient concept but still it has the important place in teacher education programmes in the teaching practices. In most of training institutions the Herbartian five steps approach of lesson planning is used.

"Johan Fredrik Herbart is a German philosopher and great Educational. He has divided teaching unit activities into five steps. His approach is theoretically based on appreciative mass theory of learning. Therefore, he gives more emphasis of teacher presentation". It appears from its structure that Classical Human Organisation Theory influences this approach. The previous knowledge of student is considered in preparing a lesson plan but their abilities, interests, attitudes and values are not taken into consideration in designing a lesson–plan. The teacher is organised at memory–level. This approach has the wider use in the teaching of various school subjects.

Under this approach the following five steps are employed:

- Preparation
- Presentation
- Comparison and abstraction
- Generalisation and
- Application.

Outline of Lesson Plan

An outline of a lesson plan has been developed on the basis of these five steps in the following forms:

- Subject, topic, class with section, period and date,
- General objectives of the teaching subject,
- Specific objectives related to the topic,
- Introduction,
- Statement of aim,
- Presentation including developing questions,
- Explanation,
- Blackboard Summary,
- Review, questions or Recapulatory questions, and
- Homework or assignment.

The above teaching points are followed in preparing teaching a lesson:

(1) Subjects, Topic and Class

A teacher selects a topic for the teaching of his own interest. He decides the data period and section of his class. These details are written in preparing his lesson plan. This step also delimits his lesson plan.

(2) General Objectives of the Teaching Subject

The different school subjects have their own general objectives. The topic is taught at different levels but these levels have different objectives. The teacher has to write the general objective of his subjects considering the level of the students. These general objectives can be achieved by organising teaching for a period of forty minutes duration.

(3) Specific Objectives

A lesson plan is prepared for achieving learning objectives, which are concerned with general objectives of teaching. The specific objectives may be knowledge skills and appreciations. The social studies lesson is designed for achieving knowledge objectives, poetry lesson for appreciation and language, craft and home science for skill. These are written in behavioural terms.

(4) Introduction

This step mainly concern with starting points of teaching activities. The teacher employs his insight and experiences for linking new knowledge with the previous knowledge of the students. Preparing introductory questions may use the priming and prompting devices. The topic is usually emitted by the student's responses by asking questions or creating appropriate situation.

(5) Statement of Aim

An introductory stage, the efforts are made for emitting the topic from the students. The teacher gives his statement of teaching topic by incorporating the student responses.

(6) Presentation

The teacher prepares developing questions after introducing the topic to be taught. The presentation is done with the help of developing questions. The questions are arranged in a logical sequence keeping in view the structure of teaching unit.

(7) Explanation

When the students are not able to answer the developing questions of teacher, he is supposed to explain the element or concept by giving the statements.

(8) Blackboard Summary

The teacher has to prepare the Blackboard summary of his teaching points and explanations.

(9) Recapulatory Questions

The students should note down the Blackboard summary. The black board summary must be removed before asking the recapulatory questions. The purpose of these questions is to practice the student learning and evaluate the student's performance to know that they could comprehend the teaching unit.

(10) Homework

At the end of lesson plan, some Homework is assigned to the students on the same topic. The purpose of Homework is to practice, to organise and to study the topic. The students get an opportunity for assimilation with the help of Homework or assignments.

Advantages of Herbartian Lesson Planning

The following are major advantages of Herbartian five steps of lesson planning:

- It is logical and psychological. It incorporates the principles of learning.

- It is employed in the teaching for all school subject social studies, languages, English and Science subjects.

- It employs the deductive and inductive method of teaching.

- It is useful for achieving the cognitive objectives of teaching.

- It is simple and easy approach of lesson planning.

- It employs the previous knowledge of the students for imparting new knowledge.

Demerits of Herbartian Lesson planning

The Herbartian lesson planning is most popular but it has the following demerits:

- It is highly dominated by the teacher.

- It is highly structured and does not provide the opportunities for learner's creativity and originality.

- It is highly located by cognitive objectives but cannot be effectively employed for affective and psychomotor objectives.

- It does not consider the learning–structures in organising teaching activities.

- The specific objectives are not written in behavioural terms.

- The teaching activities are less meaningful and practical.

(B) BLOOM'S OR EVALUATION APPROACH TO LESSON PLANNING

The evaluation approach is a new innovation in the field of education. It has revolutionized the teaching, learning and testing process. It considers that education is the tricolour process.

This approach has the following features:

- The education is a purposeful process. All the educational Activities are objective–centred.

- The testing should be based on teaching. The teaching and testing should be objective oriented.

- The term evaluation concerns with all activities of teaching and testing and not only students performances.

- It does not confine to the students achievement only but it includes the total behaviour change of the students.

- It evaluates the teaching–learning objectives, methods and devices of providing learning experiences.

- The student's performances are measured in terms of learning objectives and not the achievement of the content. It may cover cognitive, affective and psychomotor learning outcomes used.

B.S. Bloom has given this approach to teaching learning. The following three steps are:

(1) Formulating Educational Objectives,

(2) Creation Learning Experiences, and

(3) Evaluating the Change of behaviours.

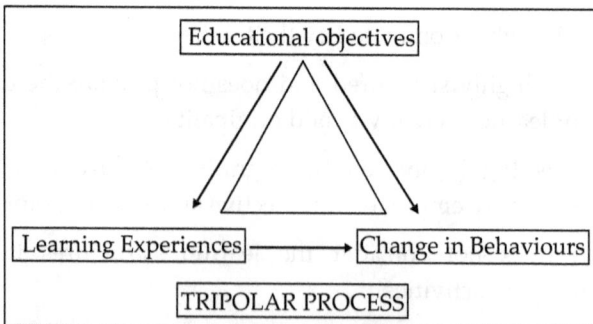

Fig. 1.1

(1) Formulating Formulation of Educational Objectives

The end result of any activity is known as objective. The well–organised activity brings a desirable change, which is termed as objective. The educational objectives concern with collative, affective and psychomotor change in the behaviours. The following things should be kept in mind in identifying and formulating educational objectives:

- The nature of various school subjects in significantly different. Thus, different objectives are achieved by teaching the various school subjects.

- The structure of the content, students level and need, social and economic conditions, practical and cultural needs are the basis for determining the objectives of teaching.

- The student's growth and development should be kept in view in formulating the objectives of learning, because the same contents are taught at different stage of development.

- The student entering behaviours and their comprehension levels are considered in formulating learning objectives.

- The objectives are written in behavioural terms after identifying them. The procedure is followed in formulating and writing objectives in behavioural form.

(2) Creating Learning Experiences

After identifying the learning objective, the appropriate teaching strategies, teaching aids and tactics are selected for generating the environments for providing the learning experiences to the students. The learning experiences are directly related to the objectives of teaching. These learning experiences may be provided in the school or classroom and outside the school. A teacher organises his/her activities for bringing the desirable change among the students. The teaching activities are related to learning outcomes. This concept has been illustrated with the help of the following way:

The table indicates that employing different type of teaching strategies for achieving different learning objectives provides different types of learning experiences.

Table 1.1

S. No.	Teaching Objectives	Learning Experiences
(1)	Knowledge Objective	Lecturing Telling, showing, demonstration, Chart, models, text book, programmed instruction, Homework, and assignments.

(2)	Understanding Objective	Question–answer strategy, group discussion, Line drawing, Map, Models, Text Books, Homework and assignments.
(3)	Application Objective	Project Method, Tutorials, Inter action strategy, Text Book, Homework, and assignments
(4)	Creativity Objective	Problem solving, Method individual experimentation, Seminar and workshop, etc.

(3) Evaluating change of Behaviours

The learning experiences bring desirable change in behaviour of the students. The change of behaviours is evaluated to take decision about the effectiveness of learning experiences. The change of behaviours is of three types: cognitive, affective and psychomotor. A criterion test is prepared for measuring all the three types of objectives. The objective and essay type tests are constructed for measuring cognitive objectives. The oral questions are used in lesson planning. The following measuring devices are used for evaluating cognitive, psychomotor and affective objectives:

Table 1.2

S. No.	Learning Objectives	Evaluation Devices
(1)	Cognitive	Oral, observation, written essay and objective type tests and interview.
(2)	Affective	Observation, interest inventory, attitude scale, value test, essay type test and situational test.
(3)	Psychomotor	Observation, practical examination, student demonstration and interview.

It is evident from the table that different types of measuring instruments and devices are employed for evaluating three types of objectives. The change of behaviour is the empirical criterion for the effective use of teaching strategies, tactics and teaching aids which have been used for providing the learning experiences.

Merits of Bloom's Lesson planning

The following are the main characteristics of lesson planning:

- The content analysis is done and two–dimensional charts are prepared for specifying the objectives.
- The objectives are written in behavioural terms.
- The teaching activities are organised for achieving these objectives.
- The teaching activities are related to the learning structures.
- This type of lesson plan makes the teaching purposeful and objective centred.

- It is based on psychological and scientific principles.
- It has the greater scope for improving and modifying the learning experience on teaching activities.

Demerits of Bloom's Lesson planning

This has the following demerits:

- This approach of lesson planning is highly structured and mechanized and does not provide an opportunity for creativity and originality of the teacher.
- It has the greater scope for personal factors of teacher influence the planning and organising teaching activities.
- One teaching activity does not confine to one domain. It concerns with more than one domain.
- The mental process or mental abilities are not taken into consideration in writing objectives in behavioural term.

(C) RCEM APPROACH TO LESSON PLANNING

The Indian educationists develop this approach of lesson planning. This is an improvement over the earlier approaches. It also considers the Bloom's Taxonomy of Educational objectives in identifying objective of teaching with certain modification. RCEM approach involves seventeen mental abilities for writing objectives in functional form.

The structure of lesson plan is developed with help of input, process and output aspects of teaching.

Input

It includes the identification of objectives. They are known as Expected Behavioural Outcomes (EBOs). These objectives are broadly classified into four categories: knowledge, understanding, application and creativity. These objectives are written in behavioural terms by employing seventeen mental abilities. The entering behaviours of the learners are also identified. The sequence of instructional procedure is determined with the help of these objectives.

Process

The teaching strategies and tactics are selected for achieving these objectives. The communication strategy and audio–visual aids are employed for the effective presentation of the content. The main focus of the process is to create the learning situations for providing appropriate learning experiences to the students. The process also includes the technique of motivation so that student's behaviour can be reinforced for the desirable responses. It implies the interaction of teacher and students. The participation of pupils and teacher is essential.

Output

This aspect of instructional procedure includes the Real Learning outcomes (RLOs). Learning experiences are provided for the desirable Behavioural change among students, the change of the behaviours is known as real learning outcomes. The various measuring devices are employed for evaluating RLOs. The measuring instruments are constructed based on EBOs. The teacher usually measures the RLOs by using oral and writing questions.

Merits of RCEM Approach

- More suitable to our schools, as it has been developed in our country.
- Use of mental processes in place of action worlds while writing the instructional objectives.
- The focus on the process, not on product while writing objectives.
- Evaluation task in quite simple and objective.

Demerits of RCEM Approach

- Time consuming approach.
- Suitable to cognitive objectives only, no dealing with affective and psychomotor objectives.
- The whole learning of human being cannot be explained fully through only 17 mental abilities.
- This approach is an improvement over the prevailing practices of lesson planning.

Limitations of Lesson Planning

- It makes teaching organised but rigid.
- If followed strictly, it leaves no room for innovativeness on the part of the teacher.
- Too much of emphasis on it may make things routinised.
- It is good for beginner teachers. Experienced teachers usually have little faith in structured classroom behaviours.
- It is difficult to anticipate all possible kinds of classroom situations in advance and therefore lesson plans lack relevance.

✍ ✍ ✍

2 Teaching of English

• • •

The world is shrinking rapidly today. Advances in information technology, scientific knowledge and applications audio–visual aids have transformed a sprawling earth into a global village. Peoples of various cultures and nationalities now meet, interact, trade and socialise with ease on a daily basis.

Making this possible is the use of a common language, i.e. English. Over 350 million people use English across the globe. Some like the Americans, Canadians and Australians use it as their mother tongue, some like Indians, Africans, Chinese, Europeans, Japanese and South Americans use it as a second language and others learn it as a foreign language.

One person out of every four persons in the world can be reached anywhere through English. 50 per cent of the world's newspapers, scientific and technical journals and over 60 per cent of the world's radio stations use English as a means of communication. It is also the official language of the United Nations Organisation (UNO).

Position of English in Free India

With the dawn of independence, a controversy began about the place, importance and study of English. People like C. Rajagopalachari favoured its retention at its place. But there were persons who under the influence to nationalism, strongly advocated that English should quit India with the English. They argued that English being a foreign language was responsible for a very great waste of students' time and energy. They declared that students could learn and express their ideas more easily in their mother tongue, i.e. Hindi. What the nationalists said had some reason in it. In free India, English could not be allowed to occupy the position of privilege. All the persons acknowledged this. Consequently, it was decided that regional languages should be developed and that Hindi should replace English. Nothing can be said against these things. Independent India must have its own national language.

Value of Teaching English

Pandit Nehru was certainly correct when he said, "English is our major window on the modern world." Its importance as an international language cannot be denied. It is only through English that we can establish social, economical, cultural and political relations with other countries of the world. It opens a wide window of international relations for us. If we close this window, we will shut ourselves up in the four walls of our nationality. This will certainly bring about our decay and downfall because modern science has reduced the vast dimensions of the globe to the size of a small bail. Under such circumstances we cannot ignore English, we should give Hindi the place of national language. But this never means that English should be completely eradicated from the Indian curriculum.

"English is a language which is rich in literature, humanistic, scientific and technical. If under sentimental urges we should give up English, we would cut our self off from the living stream of ever growing knowledge".

—University Grand Commission

"No language ancient and modern can be compared with English in the number of its speakers, writers and readers all over the world".

—F.G. French

Whatever arguments may be advanced for doing away with the teaching of English, its value and importance for us cannot be underestimated. For this, our reasons are as follows:

- English is the 'linkup Franca' of the world.
- We can exchange our views with the people of other countries through this language.
- Its study facilitates the establishment of international contact between different nations of the world.
- Its study gives an opportunity to Indians to get employment not only in India but also in other countries.
- It's very long association with Indian life that has made it a language of many Indians.
- It has given us the opportunity to study English literature that is so vast and so rich.
- It has opened the gates of Western science and technology for us. If these subjects are taught then the regional languages will lag behind in scientific knowledge.
- It has exercised a very healthy influence on Indian languages. It has developed and refined them in many ways.
- It serves as a common language of Indians, and thus, it brings closer the people residing in different parts of India. It is only through the medium of English that a man from the far north can talk to a man from the remote south in India.
- It is a language of trade and industry in India at the same time. Indian Businessmen can correspond with foreign businessmen only through the medium of English.
- It has already united Indians. It can help them further in destroying the boundary of provincialism.
- Almost all our great leaders, famous scientists, renowned philosophers and well–known authors are the products of English education.
- English is one of the most developed languages of the world. As such, it has always been a source of development in all the spheres of human activities.

- We may be able to translate English medical, scientific and technological terms into Hindi and regional languages. But if we give up the study of English we cannot keep pace with the scientific progress of the Western countries.

Based on the arguments advanced above, we can say that the value and importance of the teaching English in India cannot be denied by anyone. We have to bear in mind these words of **Champion,** *"English literature in quantity and quality is second to none in the world".*

Importance of Teaching English

The importance of teaching English in India as a modern foreign language lies in the following things:

- **International Importance:** English claims to be the first rate international language. It can even be called a universal language. Hence, it is an international language. By extending the radius of a person's horizon, it overcomes his prejudice, intolerance and narrow–mindedness. Thus, it is very helpful in fostering true international and co–operation among the nations of the world.

- **Educational Importance:** English is a direct medium of acquiring a knowledge of modern arts, science, humanities, technology, etc. It is equally important for statesmen and politicians, scientists and doctors, engineers and educationists, businessmen and research workers. They enrich their knowledge and experience by reading English books and journals. Consequently, they contribute to the progress of their underdeveloped country like India.

- **Vocational Importance:** Study of English as a modern foreign language has tremendous vocational importance for us. It offers opportunities for many and varied vocations, like diplomatic and foreign services, business, commerce, medicine, teaching law, etc.

- **Cultural Importance:** English widen one's cultural and intellectual horizon. It develops scientific, technical and commercial relation with other countries. It imparts knowledge of foreign nations and cultures. Thus, it further required mutual understanding and co–operation.

- **Disciplinary Importance:** The study of English enables a person to compare and contrast the good and bad things of his country with those of other nations. By doing so, he trains his analytical and reflective faculties. Thus, he acquires a new insight into various resources of thought and expression.

- **Recreational Importance:** English is a good source of recreation and useful employment of leisure. Persons knowing English can enjoy the best stories, drama, novels, etc. written or translated into English.

How should English be taught?

We cannot close our eyes to the importance of English as a modern foreign language. To identify it as the language of the British shows our narrow mindedness. To abhor it because our abhorred rulers thrust it upon us reveals our prejudice. We have to look to the blessings it has showered upon us. It has developed us and given us unity in diversity. Today, it is as much a language of our country as any other. It is used by the whole educated mass of Indians. It is used in administration, trade, commerce and inter–state communication. Thus, its teaching has to be continued in our schools and colleges. This can be done in the following ways:

- At the primary stage, English should not be taught.

- At the secondary stage, English should be taught as an optional subject from class VI.

- At the university stage, English should be a compulsory subject. It should not be the medium of instruction and examination, but every student should pass an examination proving his ability to read common English books and to write correctly. If it is not done, India will lag behind in the modern age of science. Moreover, there will be a dearth of Indian leadership in the international sphere.

Place of English in the School Curriculum

The British introduced the English system of education in India in 1835. It was the language used by the British administration and was thus politically imposed on the Indian Education System. English was taught as a compulsory subject.

After Independence, various changes occurred in the education system. Various Education Commissions who are appointed by the Indian Government recommended progressive switch over to the mother tongue. However, the importance of English too could not be overlooked. It is the language of the world and the knowledge of English makes a person a citizen of the world. Even if English ceases to be the medium of instruction, it continues to be taught as a subject in school curriculums. Various formulae have been devised over the years: English to be taught only from Std. VI, but is compulsory upto college level. In some schools, English is taught only from Std. VIII. Various stages have devised their own educational policies, incorporating English as a second language, or giving it the status of a foreign language. However, it continues to be taught at various levels all over the country. The Kothari Commission has recommended that the study of English as a co–language should be compulsory upto Class I. English may therefore be taught as a compulsory subject at school level and made an optional subject thereafter.

Aims of Teaching English

According to Thompson, there are four specific aims of teaching English at the school stage:

- To understand spoken English
- To speak English
- To understand written English
- To write English

To understand spoken English

At school level, the students should have the ability to understand spoken English, needed in ordinary conversation, exchange of directions and listening to lecture, talks, running commentary on matches, news bulletins, etc. on the radio and participation in school debates and dramas.

To achieve this aim, students should be given opportunities to listen English radio. Gramophone and tape recorder can also be used for this purpose. The aim should be to enable the students to understand English spoken by the native speakers.

To speak English

At second stage, speaking English is easier than reading and writing. At the same time, speaking English is more difficult than reading, as it requires the ability to produce sounds and to speak with proper stress and intonation. Speech is of unique importance in learning a language. It is the base for all language learning. This aim of teaching English is being neglected in our schools because it is not important from the examination point of view.

At the end of five or six years of learning English, we expect the students to talk fluently in English. Their speech should be fairly intelligible to the native speakers. For this purpose, tape recorders can be used. The ability to speak English is required in big cities, where people speaking different languages communicate with one another in English. This aim is important because ability to speak English is required while communicating with foreigners.

To understand written English

The third stage is to understand written English. It is very important for students. It enables them to have and access to the latest information in their subject of studies. It is expected from a school leaver in India, if he joins a college, should be able to adopt English as the medium of instruction and examination in his studies.

Aims of teaching English is to enable the students to read with understanding printed material in English. At present, students reading comprehension in English is very poor. They are not able to comprehend material published in English. The main emphases of work in English should be on reading comprehension. Early reading may be loud reading. This will prepare ground for silent reading in English in higher classes and adult life. Recognition vocabulary of students should be increased to enable them to read English with comprehension.

To write English

Writing English comes last, but it is equally important. Writing is not less important than listening, speaking and reading. One of the aims of teaching English should be to enable the school–leavers to write simple letters, applications, descriptions and accounts of events in English. The ability to write in English is needed in offices because English continues to be the language of administration at the central level. It is also the language of communication between the Center and the States and between one State and the other. The ability is also needed in college and university where one has to take notes from lecturers delivered in English as well as from the books and journals published in English. Students should be able to write English correctly and legibly.

Aims of Teaching English at Junior and Senior Levels

There are two stages at which English has to be taught:

- The junior level (classes VI, VII and VIII)
- The senior level (classes IX, X, XI and XII)

It is essential that we define aims of teaching English clearly at the junior and the senior levels.

Teaching English at the Junior Level

- *Understand English when spoken:* His standard of speech should approximate the native speaker's so that if a native speaker speaks English, which is not above his level, he should be able to understand it.
- Acquire reading ability and read the material that is appropriate for his level.
- Acquire a vocabulary, which though limited, is enough to help him in the use of the language that he makes.
- Have his aim fixed at the conversational English, as it is used in speech. Our purpose in the beginning should be to help the students in acquiring a command over spoken forms, colloquial or conversational English, rather than the textbook English.
- Make simple statements through English. He should be able to frame short, simple sentences to express himself through speech and writing.
- Speak with a pronunciation that is acceptable. He should acquire a command over the phonemes of the language and speak English with proper stress and intonation.
- Respond to short conversational questions and to ask questions himself.
- Write English legibly and coherently using proper punctuation and capitals where necessary with correct spellings.
- Use English when he has to respond to calls, requests, greetings, etc. when he has to do the same to others.

Teaching English at the Senior Level

- Students at the end of the secondary stage should be able to speak English fluently and accurately. Fluency implies acquisition of a reasonable standard in speech–habits, which means speaking with an acceptable pronunciation and intonation.
- They should be able to speak freely. They should think in English and speak it with ease and frequently.
- They should be able to talk in English and to express their ideas in English in classroom, at home and in society. They should be able to respond and react to situations actively and not remain just a passive listener.
- They should acquire the ability to understand the native speakers and also be able to respond to them.
- They should be able to compose freely and independently in speech and writing.
- They should be able to read books with understanding. They should also be able to read newspapers and periodicals.
- They should acquire a vocabulary of 2500 words approximately and that should include frequent and choicest English phrases and idioms.
- They should be able to use reference materials, i.e. encyclopaedia, dictionaries, reference books, etc. when they stand in need thereof.

Objectives of Teaching English and their Achievements

Thompson and Wyatt rightly remark that the Indian pupil should not only understand English when it is spoken or written but he should also be able to speak and write English fluently.

There are three objectives of teaching English in the secondary schools:

- To teach students to hear and understand the spoken language.
- To teach them to understand what they read.
- To teach them to write it.

To understand the spoken and the written language and to speak and write it, are the objectives of teaching English in our secondary schools. With these aims, the task of an English teacher is to train the hearing, speaking and writing abilities of the pupils. This is the linguistic aim of teaching English in schools.

Practical command of the languages has been stated to be the main aim of secondary school instruction in English as judged by the ability to write in good modern English on any simple topic without previous preparation. Hence, at the high school or senior secondary level where English is to be treated as a second language, we should be contended with its linguistic aims. Our chief concern should not be about the difficulties of pronunciation, growth of vocabulary, grammar and structure, but with language abilities.

To make the realisation of the objectives of teaching English in our secondary schools, the teachers' first concern should be to get the students' language abilities into action. The learning of a language goes with his/her activity. This fact should be the guiding principle in devising methods, plan of work and selection of schemes for the language teaching in secondary schools. During seven years of schooling in English, the English teacher is to concentrate upon training his pupils in their hearing, reading, speaking and writing only. Then, it is desirable to begin with oral work. Afterward, more opportunities for speaking and reading ought to be offered.

The teacher should bear in mind that his main task is to develop four language abilities. He should strive to the utmost and do all that his resources permit him to realise the objectives of teaching English in secondary schools. They are:

- Good teachers in our schools who are proficient in the subject and who have the necessary attitude to teach; and
- Well–organised programme, good textbooks and better student–teacher ratio.

"It is necessary that the Indian pupil should not only understand English when it is spoken or written, but also that he should himself be able to speak and write it".

–Thompson and Wyatt

Problems of Teaching English in India

The teacher of English in India faces various problems and has to teach despite various limitations. Some of these constraints are:

- Poor classroom conditions, the physical environment itself is not conducive to learn with poorly ventilated rooms. The classroom equipment is also inadequate.

- The strength of the students is quite huge and teaching a language becomes quite difficult. No individual attention can be paid.

- No audio visual aids are provided and English is taught like any other information–oriented subject.

- The purpose of teaching the language is not clear. No clear objectives for the teaching of English are conveyed.

- Different syllabi for different schools and at various levels of the teaching of English result in irregular results.

- Poorly designed textbooks, which do not use realistic situations from the students' life, also contribute to the poor quality of English education in the country today.

- Faulty methods of teaching are adopted. Instead of following the structural and situational approaches, the translation–cum–grammar approach is followed. The natural imbibing of the language and absorption of the structure and situational use of the language does not happen.

How to Solve Problems of Teaching English

- Oral work with the student reading and speaking the language has to be done. Textbooks should follow a graded vocabulary,

- Should be appropriately illustrated,

- Subject matter should be relevant, should have good language and style, an extensive glossary and well devised exercises.

- Textbooks should be accompanied with students' workbooks, teacher's handbook, supplementary readers and the necessary audio–visual aids like charts, records and tapes.

French permits the use of the mother tongue for explaining the meaning of the words, provided the teacher immediately gets back to English. Total translation of the English textbook is not permitted.

The aim of teaching the language is that the students should speak, read and write English perfectly. To this end, any written work done by the students should be corrected thoroughly and mistakes should be corrected.

The examination system should focus on the concept of mastery of the language shown in the skillful use of vocabulary and sentence structure rather than on rote learning. Fluency in spoken English should also be evaluated.

Suggestions to Improve Teaching of English

- The three–language formula should be followed with the regional language as the first language, Hindi being the national language, as the second language and English taught as the third language.

- Teachers should be trained. Summer schools, crash training programmers, workshops and seminars at regional and national levels could be held periodically to upgrade the language skills of the teachers.

- Orientation programmes, workshops, refresher courses for inspection staff should be conducted frequently.

- Textbooks should be written by experts and supplementary readers and workbooks, handbooks, audio–visual aids should be provided with them.

- Evaluation of the students' language skills should focus on vocabulary, sentence structure, work–order, use of prepositions, degrees of comparison, verb forms and tenses and on spoken language and pronunciation.

✍ ✍ ✍

(3) Different Lesson Planning

●●●

Supplementary
Reader

LESSON PLAN — 1

Tansen

Tansen was a famous singer. His father was a famous poet by the name of Mukund Mishra. Tansen was named Tannu Mishra when he was born. Tansen was born in a Hindu family in a place called Gwalior located in Madhya Pradesh. Tansen was a naughty child. He learnt to imitate the calls of birds and animals perfectly. He also used to play in the nearby forest.

One day, a famous singer named Swami Haridas was taking rest with his disciples in the forest. To frighten them, Tansen hid behind a tree and roared like a tiger. Swami Haridas did not run in fear. One of his disciples brought Tansen to Haridas. Haridas noticed the talent in Tansen who was just ten years old. He made Tansen his disciple. Tansen learnt music for eleven years. He became a great singer.

Tansen's parents died at about that time. His father's dying wish was that Tansen should visit Mohammad Ghaus, a holy man. So, Tansen started living with his father's favourite. Tansen started visiting Rani Mrignaini's court. He married a court lady named Hussaini. She also became Swami Haridas's disciple. They had five children.

Emperor Akbar appointed Tansen as his court musician. Tansen soon became his favourite. Some of the courtiers became jealous of Tansen. They wished to ruin him. Shaukat Mian had a bright idea. He knew that if a singer sang Raga Deepak properly, the singer would be burnt into ashes. One day he requested the emperor to test Tansen's musical skill. He appealed to the emperor to see if Tansen could sing this Raga Deepak. The emperor agreed. He asked Tansen to sing the raga.

Tansen was unhappy but he could not disobey the emperor. He asked the emperor to give him some time to practice the raga. The king agreed.

Tansen had an idea. He thought if someone sang Raga Megh at the same time, it would bring rain. He would be saved. He asked his daughter Saraswati and her friend Rupvati to practice singing Raga Megh.

Now, Tansen began to sing Raga Deepak on the appointed day. It became very hot. Lamps began to burn. Just then, Saraswati and her friends started Raga Megh. It began to rain. Tansen was saved. But he fell ill.

The emperor punished Tansen's enemies. Tansen got well. He remained Akbar's court singer till he died in 1585. Tansen's tomb is in Gwalior. Musicians visit the tomb to pay their respects to the greatest musician of India.

Subject: English	**Date:** _____
Topic: Tansen	**Duration:** 35 – 40 minutes
	Class: 6th

(1) General Objectives

- To enable the students to understand, write and speak English correctly.
- To enable the students to read the lesson with correct pronunciation.
- To enable the students to understand the passage and grasp its meaning.
- To develop the abilities of imagination, reasoning and observation.
- To inculcate creativity in students.

(2) Specific Objectives

To enable the students to learn about Tansen.

(3) Previous Knowledge

The students must have at least general familiarities with Tansen.

(4) Teaching Aids

Blackboard, chalk, duster, pointer, etc.

(5) Introduction

Teacher's Question	Student's Answer
(i) Have you ever heard the name of Tansen?	(i) Yes.
(ii) Who was Tansen?	(ii) Tansen was a famous singer.
(iii) Do you know about his whole life?	(iii) ....

(6) Statement of topic

Now, teacher will announce the topic, "Today, I shall teach you about Tansen".

(7) Presentation

Content	Pupil–Teacher Activity	Student's Activity
Model reading	Tansen was..............nearby forest. The pupil–teacher will read the lesson with correct pronunciation, stress and information.	The students will listen alternatively and follow him/her in their note-books.
Pronunciation drill	The pupil–teacher will write some difficult words on the blackboard and ask the students to pronounce them. These words are famous, imitate and perfectly.	A few students will pronounce these difficult words.
Exposition of difficult words	The pupil–teacher writes the word meanings and tells the students to note down in their notebooks. These are as follows: Famous: प्रसिद्ध Imitate: नकल करना Forest: जंगल Perfectly: अच्छे तरीके से	Students will note down the word meanings from the board.
Comprehension	The teacher will ask some questions: (a) What was the name of Tansen when he was born? (b) Where was Tansen born? (c) What was the name of Tansen's father?	(a) Tannu Mishra (b) Gwalior located in Madhya Pradesh (c) Mukund Mishra
Reading	Pupil–teacher will read the next paragraph One day..............great singer.	The students will listen attentively and follow him/her in their books.

	The pupil–teacher writes the word meanings and tells the students to note down in their notebooks. These are as follows: Disciple: शिष्य Behind: के पीछे Frighten: डराना Roar: दहाड़ना Talent: प्रतिभा	
Comprehension	The teacher will ask some questions: (a) Who was taking rest with his disciple? (b) When did Swami Haridas notice the talent in Tansen?	(a) Swami Haridas (b) When Tansen was just 10 years old, tried him to frighten, Swami Haridas noticed the talent in Tansen.
Silent Reading	Pupil–teacher will ask the students to read the passage silently without moving their lips and will supervise them.	The students will read the passage on their own and try to understand it.

(8) Evaluation

- Tansen was the follower of _____.
- What was the name of the Tansen's father and where did his parents live?

(9) Homework

- How do you know that Akbar was fond of Tansen? Give two reasons.
- Why did Tansen agree to sing Raga Deepak?

LESSON PLAN — 2

The Tiny Teacher

The ant is the commonest, the smallest but the wisest insect. Some people kept ants as pets. They watched the ants' behaviour closely. They discovered amazing facts about this tiny, hard-working and intelligent creature. Ants do "talk" to each other. Each ant greets all others coming from the opposite directions. They do so by touching their feelers or antennae. This is their method of passing messages.

Ants are of many kinds. Black and red ants are the commonest. Ants live in their "nests" called "anthills". An anthill has hundreds of little rooms and passages. Some rooms are for the queen to lay eggs. Others are used as nurseries for the 'grubs'. Some are reserved quarters for the workers. Workers spend most time searching for food. An ant's life is very orderly and peaceful. Each ant does its work intelligently and efficiently. No ant ever fights with other members of the groups.

Queen ant is the mother of the whole colony. It lives for fifteen years. It has a pair of wings. It bits off its wings after its 'wedding flight'. The queen meets the male ant–drone–high up in the air on a hot summer day. After this 'wedding flight', it does nothing but lays eggs.

Grubs come out of hatched eggs. They are well taken ears of and guarded. Workers feed them, clean them and also carry them about daily for airing and exercising. After two to three weeks, grubs turn into cocoons. They lie without food or activity for three weeks more. When the cocoons break, ants appear. After a few weeks of teaching and training, they join the workforce.

Some other creatures like beetles, leaser broods of ants and the greenfly also live in an anthill. Some are accepted because they emit pleasant smell. Some give sweet juices. Some are just pets. The greenfly is ants' cow. They milk it for 'honeydew' just as humans milk the cow.

Humans can learn some precious lessons from ants' lives. They can learn the lesson of hard work, sense of duty and discipline, cleanliness, care of the young ones and above all a firm loyalty to the land where they live.

Subject: English	Date: _____
Topic: The Tiny Teacher	Duration: 35 – 40 minutes
	Class: 7th

(1) General Objectives

- To enable the students to understand, write and speak English correctly.
- To enable the students to read the lesson with correct pronunciation.
- To enable the students to understand the passage and grasp its meaning.
- To develop the abilities of imagination, reasoning and observation.
- To inculcate creativity in students.

(2) Specific Objectives

To acquaint the students with the lesson "The Tiny Teacher".

(3) Previous Knowledge

The students must have at least general familiarities with a word 'ant'.

(4) Teaching Aids

Blackboard, chalk, duster, pointer, etc.

(5) Introduction

Teacher's Question	Student's Answer
(i) Have you heard a word 'ant'?	(i) Yes.
(ii) What is an ant?	(ii) An ant is a small insect.
(iii) Good, what do you know about 'ant'?	(iii) ....

(6) Statement of topic

Now, teacher will announce the topic, "Today, I shall teach you about ant."

(7) Presentation

Content	Pupil–Teacher Activity	Student's Activity
Model reading	The ant..............messages.	
	The pupil–teacher will read the lesson with correct pronunciation, stress and information.	The students will listen alternatively and follow him/her in their books.

Pronunciation drill	The pupil–teacher will write some difficult words on the blackboard and ask the students to pronounce them. These words are pets, creature, feelers and antennae.	A few students will pronounce these difficult words.
Exposition of difficult words	The pupil–teacher writes the word meanings and tells the students to note down in their notebooks. These are as follows: Pets: पालतू पशु Creature: प्राणी Feelers: स्पर्शक Antennae: कीट पतंगो को स्पर्शज्ञान कराने वाला बाल	Students will note down the word meanings from the blackboard.
Comprehension	The teacher will ask some questions: (a) What do you mean by an ant? (b) How do ants convey their messages?	(a) An ant is the commonest, smallest and wisest insect. (b) They do so by touching their feelers or antennae.
Reading	Pupil–teacher will read the next paragraph: Ants are...............the group.	The students will listen attentively and follow him in their books.
	The pupil–teacher writes the word meanings and tells the students to note down in their notebooks. These are as follows: Nests: घोंसला Anthills: बाम्बी Nurseries: संवर्धन स्थान Grubs: खाना Reserved: आरक्षित	

Comprehension	The teacher will ask some questions: (a) Which are the commonest kinds of ants? (b) Describe the organisation of anthills. (c) How can we say that ants lead an orderly and peaceful life?	(a) Black and red are the commonest kinds of ants. (b) Ants live in their "nests" called "anthills". An anthill has hundreds of little rooms and passages. Some rooms are for the queen to lay eggs. Others are used as nurseries for the 'grubs'. Some are reserved quarters for the workers. Workers spend most time searching for food. (c) Because each ant does its work intelligently and efficiently and no ant ever fights with other members of the group.
Silent reading	Pupil–teacher will ask the students to read the passage silently without moving their lips and will supervise them.	The students will read the passage on their own and try to understand it.

(8) Evaluation

- How long does it take a grub to become a complete ant?
- Why do the worker ants carry the grubs about?
- What jobs are new ants trained for?
- Mention three things we can learn from the 'tiny teacher'. Give reasons for choosing these items.

(9) Homework

- How the ants are the commonest, smallest and wisest insect?
- Why does the story of the ant's life sound almost untrue?
- What is the ants' method of 'talking' to each other?
- How does the wedding flight change the queen ant's life?
- Describe the life cycle of an ant from the egg stage to its becoming a full–grown ant.

LESSON PLAN — 3

The Selfish Giant

A giant had a larger lovely garden with soft green grass. The garden had beautiful flower plants and juicy fruits. The giant was away on a visit to his friend. For seven years, he stayed with his friend. Meanwhile, the giant's garden became the favourite playground of children.

On his return, the giant was annoyed to see children playing in his garden. He constructed a high wall around the garden and put up a notice. "Trespassers will be prosecuted". That stopped the children's entry into the giant's garden. It made the children very sad and unhappy. They pined for the happy days when they could freely play in the giant's garden for the lifelong day. After that, spring came all over the country but it did not enter the selfish giant's garden. As a result, in the giant's garden it was winter forever. Flowers did not blossom there. Little birds never sang. Snow and frost started living there the year round. Snow covered up the grass. Frost painted all the trees silver. Chilly North wind roared all day about the garden. Hailstones rattled on the castle top every day and broke most of the slates.

Spring never came in the giant's garden nor the summer. Autumn gave sweet juicy fruits all around but never once did it enter the giant's garden. The giant was baffled. He was at a loss. He could not understand why spring did not visit his garden. Sitting at the window, he would look out at his cold, white garden hoping for a change in weather. But the change never came there because the giant was too selfish and mean. Spring, summer and autumn had decided to punish him for his selfishness. So, they never came to his garden.

One morning, a miracle happened. The giant was lying awake in bed when he heard sweet music. It was a little linnet singing outside his window. To the giant it seemed like the sweetest music in the world. Then the hail stopped. North wind stopped roaring. Amazed, the giant jumped out of bed and came to the window. He saw a wonderful sight. In every tree, he could see a little child. The trees were very happy to have children back that they had covered themselves with blossoms.

Birds were singing all around. Snow had disappeared and there was soft, velvety, green grass on the ground. This all had happened because children had entered the garden through a little hole in the wall. Only in one small corner of the garden, there was winter still. A little boy stood there crying. He was too small to climb a tree. That is why the tree stood in the corner was still covered with frost and snow. Taking pity on the little child, the giant went where the child stood crying. Meanwhile all other children had run away on seeing the giant. The little boy could not see the giant because his eyes were full of tears. The giant lifted the boy gently and placed him on a branch of the tree. Next moment the tree broke into blossoms. Birds came there and started singing. The little boy placed his tiny arms round the giant's neck and kissed him. On seeing this, the other children also returned to the garden. The giant took up an axe and knocked down the wall. "It is your garden now", he told the children and he too began to play with them.

Every afternoon, after school, children came there and played with the giant. The garden had changed into the most beautiful garden in the world. Everyone came except the little boy whom the giant had lifted and placed on the tree. The giant enquired about him from the other children but no one knew where the child had come from and where he had gone. The giant missed that little child and felt very sad.

Years went by. The giant becomes very old and weak. He could no longer play with the children. Sitting in an armchair, he watched the children at plat and admired his garden. He had come to realise that children are the most beautiful flowers of all. He had also realised that winter is merely the spring asleep. It was the resting time for the flowers.

One winter morning, he saw a marvellous sight. Trees in the farthest corner of the garden were covered with lovely white blossoms. Their branches were golden. Silver fruits hung down from them. Underneath one of the trees the little boy stood, whom he had loved. Running as fast as he could, he reached the spot. On the palms of the tree, child's hands were the prints of two nails and prints of two nails on his little feet. This made the giant very angry. He asked the child who had wounded him so that the giant could kill that person with his big sword. The child simply smiled at the giant's angry question and said that those were the wounds of love. The child further said that he had come to take the giant with him so that they could play together in another garden called paradise. That afternoon when the children came into the garden to play, they found the giant lying dead under the tree, all covered with white blossoms.

Subject: English	**Date:** _____
Topic: The Selfish Giant	**Duration:** 35 – 40 minutes
	Class: 8th

(1) General Objectives

- To enable the students to understand, write and speak English correctly.
- To enable the students to read the lesson with correct pronunciation.
- To enable the students to understand the passage and grasp its meaning.
- To develop the abilities of imagination, reasoning and observation.
- To inculcate creativity in students.

(2) Specific Objectives

To acquaint the students with the lesson "The Selfish Giant".

(3) Previous Knowledge

The students must have at least general familiarities with word 'giant'.

(4) Teaching Aids

Blackboard, chalk, duster, pointer, etc.

(5) Introduction

Teacher's Question	Student's Answer
(i) Have you heard a word 'giant?'	(i) Yes.
(ii) What you know about a giant?	(ii) Large person.
(iii) Have you ever heard the story of "The Selfish Giant"?	(iii) No.

(6) Statement of topic

Now, teacher will announce the topic, "Today, I shall teach you about lesson, The Selfish Giant".

(7) Presentation

Content	Pupil–Teacher Activity	Student's Activity
Model reading	A giant.................slates. The pupil–teacher will read the lesson with	The students will listen alternatively and follow

	correct pronunciation, stress and information.	him in their books.
Pronunciation drill	The pupil–teacher will write some difficult words on the blackboard and ask the students to pronounce them. These words are annoyed, prosecuted, pined, blossom, frost, roared, hailstones, rattled and slates.	A few students will pronounce these difficult words.
Exposition of difficult words	The pupil–teacher writes the word meanings and tells the students to note down in their notebooks. These are as follows: Annoyed: नाराज Prosecuted: मुकदमा चलाना Pined: बाँधना Blossom: फूलना/खिलना Frost: पाला Roared: दहाड़ा Hailstones: छोटे गोल ओले Rattled: परेशान Slates: लकड़ी की पट्टी	Students will note down the word meanings from the blackboard.
Comprehension	The teacher will ask some questions: (a) For how many years giant stayed with his friend? (b) What did giant see when he arrived in his garden? (c) What did giant do to stop the children's entry into his garden?	(a) For seven years giant stayed with his friend. (b) He saw the children playing in the garden. (c) He constructed a high wall around the garden and put up a notice. "Trespassers will be prosecuted".
Reading	Spring never.....his garden. Pupil–teacher will read the next paragraph	The students will listen attentively and follow the teacher in their books.

	Pupil–teacher will write some words and their meanings on the blackboard are as follows: Baffled: चकराया हुआ Hoping: कूदना Selfish: स्वार्थी	Students will note down the word meaning from blackboard.
Comprehension	The teacher will ask some questions: (a) What did spring, summer and autumn do to punish giant for his selfishness? (b) What was the reaction of giant after this situation? (c) Was the giant happy or sad over the state of the garden?	(a) Spring never came in the giant's garden, nor the summer. Autumn gave sweet juicy fruits all around but never once did it enter the giant's garden. (b) The giant was baffled. He was at a loss. He could not understand why spring did not visit his garden. (c) Sad.
Silent Reading	Pupil–teacher will ask the students to read the passage silently without moving their lips and will supervise them.	The students will read the passage on their own and try to understand it.

(8) Evaluation
- Why was the giant called selfish?
- Why was giant unhappy?

(9) Homework
- Why was it still winter in one corner of the garden?
- Describe the first meeting of the little boy and the giant.
- Describe their second meeting after a long interval.

LESSON PLAN — 4

The Adventures of Toto

The narrator's grandfather loved animals. He had his own private zoo. He bought a baby monkey from a tonga–driver and named it Toto. He wanted Toto to add to his collection for the zoo. The narrator's grandmother did not like his pets. Toto's presence was kept as a secret. Toto was a mischievous monkey. It was kept in a little closet, which opened into the narrator's room. Toto tore off author's school blazer. He peeled off the plaster also. Toto was kept with other animals. There he did not allow them to live peacefully.

The grandfather had to collect his pension from Saharanpur. He took Toto with him. He had to pay extra fare for Toto. Toto was ultimately accepted by the family. He was put into a stable with Nana, the family donkey. Toto teased Nana. Toto and Nana never became friends.

Once Toto nearly boiled himself alive. He used to take bath in warm water. One day, a large kitchen kettle had been left on fire to boil for tea. Toto entered the kettle. Soon the water began to boil. Toto raised himself. It was cold outside. He sat down again. He continued hopping up and down till the grandmother came to rescue him.

Toto did not give up his mischiefs. He tore things to pieces. He tore up the dresses of the aunt. He broke plates and utensils. One day he entered the dining room and ran out with a plate of pulao. After finishing the pulao, he threw the plate at the grandmother.

Toto caused much loss to the family. They could not tolerate him anymore. In frustration, the grandfather sold Toto back to the tonga–driver and heaved a sigh of relief.

Subject: English	Date: _____
Topic: The Adventures of Toto	Duration: 35 – 40 minutes
	Class: 9th

(1) General Objectives

- To enable the students to understand, write and speak English correctly.
- To enable the students to read the lesson with correct pronunciation.
- To enable the students to understand the passage and grasp its meaning.
- To develop the abilities of imagination, reasoning and observation.
- To inculcate creativity in students.

(2) Specific Objectives

To acquaint the students with the lesson "The Adventures of Toto".

(3) Previous Knowledge

The students must have at least general familiarities with zoo.

(4) Teaching Aids

Blackboard, chalk, duster, pointer, etc.

(5) Introduction

Teacher's Question	Student's Answer
(i) Do you know about zoo?	(i) Yes, zoo is a park or an institution in which living animals are kept and usually exhibited to the public.
(ii) Good, have you ever seen a baby monkey?	(ii) Yes, we have seen baby monkey.
(iii) Have you heard the story of "The Adventures of Toto"?	(iii) No.

(6) Statement of topic

Now, teacher will announce the topic, "Today, I shall teach you about lesson, The Adventures of Toto".

(7) Presentation

Content	Pupil–Teacher Activity	Student's Activity
Model reading	The narrator's …. kept a secret. The pupil–teacher will read the lesson with correct pronunciation, stress and information.	The students will listen alternatively and follow him/her in their books.
Pronunciation drill	The pupil–teacher will write some difficult words on the blackboard and ask the students to pronounce them. These words are private, collection, pets and secret.	A few students will pronounce these difficult words.
Exposition of difficult words	The pupil–teacher writes the word meanings and tells the students to note down in their notebooks. These are as follows: Private: निजी Collection: संग्रहण Pets: पालतू पशु Secret: रहस्य	Students note down the word meanings from the board.
Comprehension	The teacher will ask some questions: (a) How does Toto come to grandfather's private zoo?	(a) Grandfather is an animal lover. He had his own private zoo. He bought a baby monkey from a tonga–driver and named it Toto. He wanted Toto to add to his collection for the zoo. So he buys it and adds it to his private zoo.

	(b) Why did grandfather hide him for some time?	(b) The narrator's grand-mother did not like pets. Therefore, Toto's presence was kept as a secret.
Reading	Toto was..........live peacefully. Pupil–teacher will read the next paragraph.	The students will listen attentively and follow the teacher in their books.
	Pupil–teacher writes some words and their meanings on the blackboard are as follows: Mischievous: शरारती Closet: अलमारी Tore: काट कर अलग करना Blazer: रंगीन जाकेट Peeled: छिलना	
Comprehension	The teacher will ask some questions: (a) Where Toto was placed? (b) How did Toto behave?	(a) It was kept in a little closet, which opened into the narrator's room. (b) Toto tore off author's school blazer. He peeled off the plaster also.
Silent reading	Pupil–teacher will ask the students to read the passage silently without moving their lips and will supervise them.	The students will read the passage on their own and try to understand it.

(8) Evaluation

- Describe Toto's journey to Saharanpur.
- How did Toto behave with Nana, the donkey?

- What happened when Toto found a dish of pulao on the dining table?

(9) Homework

- How did Toto take his bath?
- Why did Toto enter the large kitchen kettle?

LESSON PLAN — 5

The Necklace

Matilda, the pretty young lady, was born in a family of clerks. She was married to a petty clerk in the office of the Board of Education. She felt that she was born for luxuries but she was suffering from poverty. This made her constantly unhappy and complaining. She wanted to have elegant dinners in shining silver, wanted to wear frocks and nice jewellery.

One day her husband Loisel got an invitation to a dance party from the Minister of Public Instruction for both of them. Monsieur Loisel was elated to receive it, but Matilda, his wife was irritated and throws down the invitation card. Tears rolled down her cheeks. Her husband kept inquiring. Finally, she said that she did not have a proper dress or jewellery. She did not want to be single out amidst the elite gathering. Finally, after a lot of thinking, her husband gave her the money to buy a new dress for her. He had kept this money for buying a gun. The dress got ready, but Matilda was still not happy because she did not have the jewels to go with it. She did not take to the idea of wearing flower jewellery. Finally, her husband in desperation suggested that she should go to Madame Forestier, her friend and borrow some of her jewellery.

Matilda went to Madame Forestier and borrowed a diamond necklace. Madame Loisel danced at the ball (party) with enthusiasm and happiness. She turned out to be the prettiest of all–elegant, gracious, smiling and full of joy. All the men noticed her, asked her name and wanted to be presented. She went home at 4 a.m. fully satisfied. Her husband was tired and remembered that he had to go to office in the morning.

She removed the wraps from her shoulders before the glass, for a final view of herself in her glory. Suddenly, she was shocked to see that the necklace was not there around her neck.

Monsieur Loisel and Mme Loisel looked in the folds of the dress and in the pockets. They could not find the necklace. He reported the matter to the police and put an advertisement in the newspapers without any result. They somehow deferred the plan of returning the necklace by a week–by writing to Mme Forestier that the clasp of the necklace had broken. They would get it repaired and return it. At the end of the week, it was not found. They decided to buy a new one.

In a shop of the Palaise–Royal, they found an exact looking necklace valued at forty thousand francs. They could get it for thirty–six thousand francs.

Loisel had only eighteen thousand francs, so he borrowed the rest from usurer and a whole race of lenders. They paid thirty–six francs to the shop to buy the necklace. It was soon given to Mme Forestier. The saving spree began. The Loisels sent away the maid, they lived in a rented room in an attic. Mme Loisel did all the household work. Monsieur Loisel also worked overtime to save money. It was a horrible life of necessity they were leading for the next ten years. Mrs. Loisel looked old.

One day Mme Loisel happened to meet Mme Forestier while she was taking a walk. She (Matilda) told her how they had replaced her necklace. They had led a miserable life because they had to repay the loan they had taken to buy her diamond necklace, which was lost by them. Mme Forestier revealed that her necklace was false and was worth only five hundred francs.

Subject: English	Date: _____
Topic: The Necklace	Duration: 35 – 40 minutes
	Class: 10th

(1) General Objectives

- To enable the students to understand, write and speak English correctly.
- To enable the students to read the lesson with correct pronunciation.
- To enable the students to understand the passage and grasp its meaning.
- To develop the abilities of imagination, reasoning and observation.
- To inculcate creativity in students.

(2) Specific Objectives

To acquaint the students with the lesson "The Necklace".

(3) Previous Knowledge

The students must have at least general familiarities with Necklace.

(4) Teaching Aids

Blackboard, chalk, duster, pointer, etc.

(5) Introduction

Teacher's Question	Student's Answer
(i) Do you know about necklace?	(i) Yes, a necklace is an article of jewellery worn around neck.
(ii) Good, have you ever seen a necklace?	(ii) Yes.
(iii) Have you heard the story of "The Necklace"?	(iii) No.

(6) Statement of topic

Now, teacher will announce the topic, "Today, I shall teach you about lesson, The Necklace".

(7) Presentation

Content	Pupil–Teacher Activity	Student's Activity
Model reading	Matalida .... nice jewellery. The pupil–teacher will read the lesson with correct pronunciation, stress and information.	The students will listen alternatively and follow him/her in their books.
Pronunciation drill	The pupil–teacher will write some difficult words on the black-board and ask the students to pronounce them. These words are pretty, clerks, petty, luxuries, poverty, constantly and elegant.	A few students will pronounce these difficult words.
Exposition of difficult words	The pupil–teacher writes the word meanings and tells the students to note down in their notebooks.	Students note down the word meanings from the board.

	These are as follows: Pretty: मनोहर Clerks: लेखाकार Petty: निर्दयी और मतलबी Luxuries: आनंद Poverty: गरीबी Constantly: लगातार Elegant: सुरुचिपूर्ण	
Comprehension	The teacher will ask some questions: (a) What kind of a person is Matilda? Why is she always unhappy?	(a) Matilda was the pretty young and simple lady born in a family of clerks. She was married to a petty clerk in the office of the Board of Education. She felt that she was born for luxuries but she was suffering from poverty. This made her constantly unhappy and complaining.
	(b) What does Matilda want in her life?	(b) She wanted to have elegant dinners in shining silver, wanted to wear frocks and nice jewellery.
Reading	One day .... her jewellery. Pupil–teacher will read the next paragraph	The students will listen attentively and follow him in their books.

	Pupil–teacher writes some words and meanings on the blackboard, which are as follows: Elated: प्रफुल्लित Irritated: उत्ते Amidst: के बीच Elite: विशिष्ट वर्ग Gathering: सभा Desperation: निराशा	
Comprehension	The teacher will ask some questions: (a) What problem disturbs Matilda?	(a) She did not have a proper dress or jewellery. She did not want to be single out amidst the elite gathering.
	(b) What was Loisel's reaction to her desire for a new dress?	(b) Her husband gave her the money to buy a new dress for her. He had kept this money for buying a gun.
	(c) Why Matilda was still not happy?	(c) Because she did not have the jewels to go with it. She did not take to the idea of wearing flower jewellery.
	(d) Finally, what did her husband suggest?	(d) Finally, her husband in desperation suggested that she should go to Mme Forestier, her friend and borrow some of her jewellery.

Silent Reading	Pupil–teacher will ask the students to read the passage silently without moving their lips and will supervise them.	The students will read the passage on their own and try to understand it.

(8) Evaluation

- What do Monsieur and Madame Loisel do next?
- How do they replace the necklace?
- The course of the Loisels' life changed due to the necklace. Comment.
- What was the cause of Matilda's ruin? How could she have avoided it?
- What would have happened to Matilda if she had confessed to her friend that she had lost her necklace?

(9) Homework

- If you were caught in a situation like Matilda, how would you have dealt with it?
- The characters in this story speak in English. Do you think this is their language? What clues are there in the story, which tell about the language and its characters?

_____ *Poetry* _____

LESSON PLAN — 6

Beauty

Beauty is seen
In the sunlight,
The trees, the birds,
Corn growing and people working
Or dancing for their harvest.
Beauty is heard
In the night,
Wind sighing, rain falling,
Or a singer chanting
Anything in earnest.
Beauty is in yourself.
Good deeds, happy thoughts
That repeat themselves
In your dreams,
In your work,
And even in your rest.

—E–YEH–SHURE

Subject: English	Date: _____
Topic: Beauty	Duration: 35 – 40 minutes
	Class: 6th

(1) General Objectives

- To enable the students to understand, write and speak English correctly.
- To develop the abilities of imagination, reasoning, aesthetic and observation.
- To enable the students to read poems aloud with proper rhythm and intonation.
- To enable the students to develop their emotions.
- To create a love for English literature in the students.

(2) Specific Objectives

- To enable the students to appreciate the poem "Beauty" written by E–Yeh–Shure.
- To enable them to understand the central idea of the poem "Beauty".
- To develop the speaking and writing skills by explaining the poem in their own sentences.

(3) Previous Knowledge

The students have already studied some poems. They can understand simple English, able to feel beauty and know the meaning of 'beauty'.

(4) Teaching Aids

Blackboard, chalk, duster, pointer, etc.

(5) Introduction

Teacher's Question	Student's Answer
(i) Do you hear the word 'beauty'?	(i) Yes, we have heard the word 'beauty'.
(ii) What can you say about it?	(ii) Quality that gives pleasure to mind or senses.
(iii) How can beauty be in yourself?	(iii) ....

(6) Statement of topic

Now, teacher will announce the topic, "Today we shall study the poem "Beauty".

(7) Presentation

Content	Pupil–Teacher Activity	Student's Activity
Model reading	Beauty is.................your rest. The teacher will read the whole poem aloud with proper expression and proper attention to rhyme and rhythm.	The students will listen alternatively and follow him/her in their books.
Exposition of Words and Phrases	The pupil–teacher writes the word meanings and tells the students to note down in their notebooks. These are as follows: Corn: बीज Sighing: आह भरना Chanting: गाना Earnest: दृढ़ Deeds: काम	Students note down these word meanings in their notebooks and try to understand them.
Explanation	The teacher will read the poem aloud with proper expression, rhyme and intonation and explain the poem in the simplest words.	The students will listen carefully and try to understand.
Appreciation	(a) Find three words in the first stanza that appeal to our sense of sight. (b) How does the poet define beauty?	(a) Sunlight, trees and birds. (b) Beauty lies in the objects of nature. All good things, good actions and all that pleases are beautiful.

	(c) How can be the "beauty is in yourself"?	(c) We can feel beauty in ourselves. Noble deeds make us beautiful.
	(d) Which objects of nature are beautiful?	(d) The singing wind and the rainfall are beautiful.
	(e) Where does beauty lie?	(e) Beauty lies in happy thoughts and good deeds.
Comprehension	The teacher will ask some questions:	
	(a) What do we see in sunlight?	(a) We see beauty.
	(b) Why do people dance for their harvest?	(b) They dance because they are pleased to harvest their crops.
	(c) Can you name some beautiful things seen or heard?	(c) Yes, we have seen the beautiful things like chirping birds, whistling trees, laughing children, vast seashore, etc.
	(d) When is the beauty heard and in which form?	(d) Beauty is heard in the night in the form of whistling of wind, rain falling and playing music.
	(e) Which things repeat in one's mind?	(e) Happy thoughts and good deeds repeat in our mind during nights.
Silent Reading	Pupil–teacher will ask the students to read the poem silently without moving their lips and fingers on the page and will supervise them.	The students will read the poem on their own and try to understand it.

(8) Evaluation

Write a paragraph about beauty. Use your own ideas along with the ideas in the poem. (You may discuss your ideas with your partner.)

(9) Homework

- The students will be asked to memorise the poem.
- What is the central idea of the poem? Explain it in your own words.

LESSON PLAN — 7

Garden Snake

I saw a snake and ran away...
Some snakes are dangerous, they say,
But mother says that kind is good,
And eats up insects for his food.
So when he wiggles in the grass
I'll stand aside and watch him pass,
And tell myself, "There's no mistake,
It's just a harmless garden snake!"

– MURIEL L. SONNE

Subject: English	**Date:** _____
Topic: Garden Snake	**Duration:** 35 – 40 minutes
	Class: 7th

(1) General Objectives

- To enable the students to understand, write and speak English correctly.
- To develop the abilities of imagination, reasoning, aesthetic and observation.
- To enable the students to read poems aloud with proper rhythm and intonation.
- To enable the students to develop their emotions.
- To create a love for English literature in the students.

(2) Specific Objectives

- To enable the students to appreciate the poem "Garden Snake" written by Muriel L. Sonne.
- To enable them to understand the central idea of the poem "Garden Snake".

- To develop the speaking and writing skill by explaining the poem in their own sentences.

(3) Previous Knowledge

The students have already studied some poems. They can understand simple English and have seen a snake.

(4) Teaching Aids

Blackboard, chalk, duster, pointer, etc.

(5) Introduction

Teacher's Question	Student's Answer
(i) Have you ever seen a snake?	(i) Yes.
(ii) Have you ever seen a snake fighting with a mongoose, getting into a hole or swimming in the river?	(ii) Yes.
(iii) Do you fear after seeing them?	(iii) Yes, because they are dangerous.
(iv)Do you ever see a garden snake?	(iv) Yes.
(v) Do you heard the story of "Garden Snake"?	(v) No.

(6) Statement of topic

Now, teacher will announce the topic, "Today, we shall study the poem "Garden Snake".

(7) Presentation

Content	Pupil–Teacher Activity	Student's Activity
Model reading	I saw……..................garden snake. The teacher will read the whole poem aloud with proper expression and proper attention to rhyme and rhythm.	The students will listen alternatively and follow him/her in their books.
Exposition of Words and	The pupil–teacher writes the word meanings and tells the students to note	Students note down these words and meanings in their

Phrases	down in their notebooks. These are as follows: Ran away: भाग गया Wiggles: हिलना Aside: अलग रखना Harmless: हानि रहित	notebooks and try to understand them.
Explanation	The teacher will read the poem aloud with proper expression, rhyme and intonation and explain the poem in simple words.	The students will listen carefully and try to understand it.
Appreciation	(a) Pick out the line, which suggests that the child is afraid of snakes. (b) Find the word that refers to the snake's movement in the grass. (c) There are four pairs of rhyming words in the poem. Write them.	(a) The line is—"I'll stand aside and watch him pass." (b) Wiggles (c) Four pairs of rhyming words are say–away, good–food, grass–pass and mistake–snake.
Comprehension	The teacher will ask some questions: (a) Name the poem and the poet. (b) What will the poet do when he sees a snake pass and why? (c) What was poet's mother said about garden snake?	 (a) The name of the poem is Garden Snake and the name of the poet is Muriel L. Sonne. (b) He will stand aside and watch him pass because he thinks that snakes are dangerous. (c) She said that garden snakes are of good kinds, they eat up insects for his food. These are harmless.

Silent Reading	Pupil–teacher will ask the students to read the poem silently without moving their lips and fingers on the page and will supervise them.	The students will read the poem on their own and try to understand it.

(8) Evaluation

- Which line shows a complete change of the child's attitude towards snakes? Read it aloud.
- "But mother says that kind is good..." What is mother referring to?

(9) Homework

- The students will be asked to memorise the poem.
- What is the central idea of the poem? Explain it in your own words.

LESSON PLAN — 8

On the Grasshopper and Cricket

The poetry of earth is never dead:
When all the birds are faint with the hot sun,
And hide in cooling trees, a voice will run
From hedge to hedge about the new–mown mead,
That is the grasshopper's — he takes the lead
In summer luxury — he has never done
With his delights, for when tired out with fun
He rests at ease beneath some pleasant weed.
The poetry of earth is ceasing never:
On a lone winter evening when the frost
Has wrought a silence, from the stone there shrills
The cricket's song, in warmth increasing ever,
And seems to one in drowsiness half lost;
The grasshopper's among some grassy hills.

–JOHN KEATS

Subject: English	**Date:** _____
Topic: On The Grasshopper and Cricket	**Duration:** 35 – 40 minutes
	Class: 8th

(1) General Objectives

- To enable the students to understand, write and speak English correctly.
- To develop the abilities of imagination, reasoning, aesthetic and observation.
- To enable the students to read poems aloud with proper rhythm and intonation.
- To enable the students to develop their emotions.
- To create a love for English literature in the students.

(2) Specific Objectives

- To enable the students to appreciate the poem "On the grasshopper and cricket" written by John Keats.
- To enable them to understand the central idea of the poem "On the grasshopper and cricket".
- To develop the speaking and writing skills by explaining the poem in their own sentences.

(3) Previous Knowledge

The students have already studied some poems. They can understand simple English.

(4) Teaching Aids

Blackboard, chalk, duster, pointer, etc.

(5) Introduction

Teacher's Question	Student's Answer
(i) Tell me the name of different seasons.	(i) Summer, Winter, Autumn and Rainy.
(ii) What do you learn from season?	(ii) ....
(iii) Do you ever hear any poem titled "On the grasshopper and cricket"?	(iii) No.

(6) Statement of topic

Now, teacher will announces the topic, "Today, we shall study the poem "On the grasshopper and cricket".

(7) Presentation

Content	Pupil–Teacher Activity	Student's Activity
Model reading	The poetry...........grassy hills.	
	The teacher will read the whole poem aloud with proper expression and proper attention to rhyme and rhythm.	The students will listen alternatively and follow him in their books.

Exposition of Words and Phrases	The pupil–teacher writes the word meanings and tells the students to note down in their notebooks. These are as follows: Hedge: घेरना Mown: काटना Mead: घास का मैदान Grasshopper: टिड्डा Luxury: सुख–साधन Delight: खुशी Beneath: नीचे की ओर Pleasant: सुहाना Ceasing: अंत होना Frost: पाले से ढक जाना Wrought: बनाया हुआ Warmth: उत्साह Drowsiness: ऊँघ/सुस्ती	Students note down these words and meanings in their notebooks and try to understand them.
Explanation	The teacher will read the poem aloud with proper expression, rhyme and intonation and explain the poem in simple English.	The students will listen it carefully and try to understand.
Appreciation	(a) By 'the poetry of the earth', what does the poet means? (b) Why the birds hide in trees? (c) Which word in stanza 2 is opposite in meaning to 'the frost'? (d) Which two seasons are mentioned in poem?	(a) The poet means the pleasures of life. (b) The birds hide in the trees because of heat. (c) warmth (d) Summer and Winter

Comprehension	The teacher will ask some questions: (a) Name the poem and the poet. (b) Write any three pairs of rhyming words from the poem.	(a) The name of the poem is "On the grasshopper and cricket", written by John Keats. (b) The three pairs of rhyming words are sun–run, mead–lead and done–fun
Silent Reading	Pupil–teacher will ask the students to read the poem silently without moving their lips and fingers on the page and will supervise them.	The students will read the poem on their own and try to understand it.

(8) Evaluation

- 'The poetry of earth' is not made of words. What is it made of (as suggested in the poem)?
- Find the lines of poem that match the following:
  - (a) The grasshopper's happiness never comes to an end.
  - (b) The cricket's song has a warmth that never decreases.

(9) Homework

- The students will be asked to memorise the poem.
- What is the central idea of the poem? Explain it in your own words.

Prose

LESSON PLAN — 9

My Childhood

Abdul Kalam is one of the world's greatest scientists. He was born in a middle–class Muslim family in 1931 at Rameswaram. His journey from a middle–class family in Rameswaram to the President's House has not been a smooth ride. He worked hard and faced all the odds of life. He was born in a conservative society. His family, his teachers and his friends influenced him in his childhood. His father, Jainulabdeen, was not much educated but he was very generous and a kind person. He was not rich but he provided Abdul a happy and secure childhood. Abdul inherited honesty and self–discipline from his father.

Abdul earned his first wages by working as a helping hand to his cousin, Samsuddin who distributed newspapers in Rameswaram.

Apart from his parents, he was also influenced by some of his friends and teachers. He had three close friends, Ramanadha Sastry, Arvindan and Sivaprakasan. Once when he was in the fifth standard, a new teacher asked him not to sit in the front row along with the high caste Brahmin boys. Abdul found Ramanadha Sastry weeping as he went to the last row. This made a lasting impression on Abdul.

Abdul was deeply influenced by his science teacher, Sivasubramania Iyer. Abdul learnt the lesson of breaking social barriers from him. Iyer invited Abdul to his home for a meal. His wife was an orthodox Brahmin. She refused to serve a Muslim boy in her pure kitchen. Iyer served Abdul with his own hands and sat down beside him to eat his meal. He convinced his wife to serve meal with her own hands.

Now Abdul was grown up. His father permitted him for higher studies and sent him to the district headquarters in Ramanathapuram. His father remarked, "Abdul! I know you have to go away and grow". And thus, began his journey.

Subject: English	Date: _____
Topic: My Childhood	Duration: 35 – 40 minutes
	Class: 9th

(1) General Objectives
- To enable the students to understand, write and speak English correctly.
- To enable the students to read the lesson with correct pronunciation.
- To enable the students to understand the passage and grasp its meaning.
- To develop the abilities of imagination, reasoning and observation.
- To inculcate creativity in students.

(2) Specific Objectives
To acquaint the students with the lesson "My Childhood".

(3) Previous Knowledge
The students must have at least general familiarity with A.P.J. Abdul Kalam.

(4) Teaching Aids
Blackboard, chalk, duster, pointer, etc.

(5) Introduction

Teacher's Question	Student's Answer
(i) Have you ever heard the name of A.P.J. Abdul Kalam?	(i) Yes.
(ii) Who was he?	(ii) He was a scientist and 11th president of India.
(iii) Good, have you read the prose of the lesson "My Childhood"?	(iii) No.

(6) Statement of topic
Now, teacher will announce the topic, "Today, I shall teach you about the lesson, My Childhood".

(7) Presentation

Content	Pupil–Teacher Activity	Student's Activity
Model reading	Abdul Kalam.... his journey.	
	The pupil–teacher will read the lesson with correct pronunciation, stress and information.	The students will listen alternatively and follow him/her in their books.

Pronunciation drill	The pupil–teacher will write some difficult words on the blackboard and ask the students to pronounce them. These words are influenced, conservative, inherited, weeping, impression, orthodox and refused.	A few students will pronounce these difficult words.
Exposition of difficult words	The pupil–teacher writes the word meanings and tells the students to note down in their notebooks. These are as follows: Influenced: प्रभाव डाला Conservative: रुढ़िवादी Inherited: वंशागत Weeping: विलाप Impression: प्रभाव Orthodox: परंपरागत Refused: अस्वीकार किया	Students will note down the word meanings from the board.
Silent Reading	Pupil–teacher will ask the students to read the passage silently without moving their lips and fingers on the page and will supervise them.	The students will read the passage on their own and try to understand it.
Comprehension	The teacher will ask some questions: (a) When and where was Abdul Kalam born? (b) Who were Abdul Kalam's school friends? (c) How did Abdul Kalam	(a) He was born in a middle–class Muslim family in 1931 at Rameswaram. (b) Ramanadha Sastry, Arvindan and Sivaprakasan (c) Abdul earned his first

	earn his first wages?	wages by working as a helping hand to his cousin, Samsuddin who distributed newspaper in Rameswaram.
	(d) What characteristics did Abdul inherit from his father?	(d) His father, Jainulabdeen, was very generous and a kind person. Abdul inherited honesty and self–discipline from his father.
	(e) What did the new teacher do in the classroom?	(e) A new teacher asked him not to sit in the front row along with the high caste Brahmin boys.
	(f) What did Abdul find after the incidents of new teacher's behaviour in the classroom?	(f) Abdul found Ramanadha Sastry weeping as he went to the last row.
	(g) What lesson did Abdul learn from his science teacher Sivasubramania Iyer?	(g) Abdul learnt the lesson of breaking social barriers from him.
	(h) Give a brief character sketch of Iyer's wife.	(h) Iyer's wife was an orthodox Brahmin. She refused to serve a Muslim boy in her pure kitchen. After convinced by her husband Iyer, She agreed to serve meal to Abdul with her own hands.
	(i) What did Abdul's father say when he sent Abdul to the district headquarters in Ramanathapuram?	(i) His father remarked, "Abdul! I know you have to go away and grow."

(8) Evaluation

- How does the author describe: (i) his father, (ii) himself?
- Give a brief character sketch of Sivasubramania Iyer.

(9) Homework

- Write the synonym of orthodox and inherited.
- You are Abdul Kalam. You were disturbed by the behaviour of the new teacher in the class. Write a page of diary expressing your feelings.

LESSON PLAN — 10

From the Diary of Anne Frank

Anne, a thirteen–year–old girl, a native of Frankfurt in Germany was born on 12th June 1929. She had to stay with her grandmother when she was only four years old. After some time, she joined her parents in Holland and was sent to a Montessori school. Later her grandmother died, which saddened her. She was a mature and intelligent girl. Through her experience in life, she learned to maintain a diary, feeling that paper has more patience than people. She was so fond of her diary that she called it Kitty. She felt she could confide in Kitty comfortably.

She was doing well in all the subjects except math. The math teacher Mr. Keesing was much annoyed with her because of her non–stop talking through the lessons. He asked her to write an essay on 'A Chatterbox' which she wrote justifying her habit as an inherited one. She felt that her habit was incurable. Again, the teacher asked her to write an essay on 'Quack, Quack, Quack, said Mistress Chatterbox'. With her friend Sanne, she wrote a poem about a father swan and three baby ducklings. The father bit the babies to death because they quacked too much. That poem changed the teacher's opinion about her and he never assigned any extra homework to her as a punishment.

Subject: English	**Date:** _____
Topic: From the Diary of Anne Frank	**Duration:** 35 – 40 minutes
	Class: 10th

(1) General Objectives

- To enable the students to understand, write and speak English correctly.
- To enable the students to read the lesson with correct pronunciation.
- To enable the students to understand the passage and grasp its meaning.

- To develop the abilities of imagination, reasoning and observation.
- To inculcate creativity in students.

(2) Specific Objectives

To acquaint the students with the lesson "From the Diary of Anne Frank".

(3) Previous Knowledge

The students must have at least general familiarities with the importance of writing a dairy.

(4) Teaching Aids

Blackboard, chalk, duster, pointer, etc.

(5) Introduction

Teacher's Question	Student's Answer
(i) Discuss the importance of writing a diary.	(i) It keeps track of every moment of life whether it is big or small.
(ii) Good, have you listen the story of "From the Diary of Anne Frank"?	(ii) No.

(6) Statement of topic

Now, teacher will announce the topic, "Today, I shall teach you about lesson, From the Diary of Anne Frank".

(7) Presentation

Content	Pupil–Teacher Activity	Student's Activity
Model reading	Anne, a ....punishment. The pupil–teacher will read the lesson with correct pronunciation, stress and information.	The students will listen alternatively and follow him in their books.
Pronunciation drill	The pupil–teacher will write some difficult words on the blackboard and ask the students to pronounce them. These words are	A few students will pronounce these difficult words.

	native, saddened, patience, confide, annoyed, inherited, incurable, swan and ducklings.	
Exposition of difficult words	The pupil–teacher writes the word meanings and tells the students to note down in their notebooks. These are as follows: Native: देशी Saddened: दुखी होना Patience: सहनशीलता Confide: बताना Annoyed: नाराज Inherited: वंशागत Incurable: असाध्य Swan: बतख Duckling: बत्तख का बच्चा	Students note down the word meanings from the board.
Silent Reading	Pupil–teacher will ask the students to read the passage silently without moving their lips and fingers on the page and will supervise them.	The students will read the passage on their own and try to understand it.
Comprehension	The teacher will ask some questions: (a) When was Anne born?	
		(a) Anne was born on 12th June 1929.
	(b) With whom she stayed before going to Holland?	(b) She had to stay with her grandmother.
	(c) What prompted Anne to maintain a diary?	(c) Through her experience in life, she learned to maintain a dairy, feeling that paper has more patience than people.
	(d) Who became Anne's friend and what was the friend's name?	(d) A diary became Anne's friend and she called it Kitty.

	(e) Why was Mr. Keesing annoyed Anne? What did he ask her to do?	(e) Mr. Keesing was much annoyed with her because of her non–stop talking through the lessons. He asked her to write an essay on 'A Chatterbox'.
	(f) How did Anne justify her being a chatterbox in her essay?	(f) She wrote justifying her habit as an inherited one. She felt that her habit was incurable.
	(g) Again, what did she write when the teacher asked her to write an essay on Quack, Quack, Quack?	(g) She wrote a poem about a father swan and three baby ducklings. The father bit the babies to death because they quacked too much.
	(h) What did Mr. Keesing do after this?	(h) He never assigned any extra homework to her.

(8) Evaluation

- In which school Anne was sent?
- Write a brief character sketch of Anne.

(9) Homework

- Why did Anne think that she was alone? Give reasons.
- How do you know that Anne was close to her grandmother?

Grammar

LESSON PLAN — 11

Subject: English	Date: _____
Topic: Kinds of Noun	Duration: 35 – 40 minutes
	Class: 6th

(1) General Objectives

- To enable the students to understand, write and speak English correctly.
- To develop communication skills of the students.
- To develop the vocabulary and language style.
- To enable them to get knowledge contained in the lesson.
- To inculcate creativity in students.

(2) Specific Objectives

- To enable the students to learn about kinds of noun.
- To enable the students to pick out various kinds of noun.

(3) Previous Knowledge

The students must have knowledge about sentence, kinds of sentences, parts of speech and they can simply define noun.

(4) Teaching Aids

Blackboard, chalk, duster, pointer, etc.

(5) Introduction

Teacher's Question	Student's Answer
(i) What do you know about a sentence?	(i) A group of words, which make complete sense.
(ii) Good, well tell me about its kinds.	(ii) Sentence is of four kinds, i.e. assertive sentence, interrogative sentence, imperative sentence and exclamatory sentence.
(iii) What do you know about parts of speech?	(iii) Noun, adjective, pronoun, verb, adverb, preposition, conjunction and interjection are parts of speech.

(iv) Good, define noun with examples.	(iv) It is a word used as the name of a person, place or thing as, Vikas is an intelligent boy. Shruti is a lazy girl.
(v) What are different types of noun?	(v) ....

(6) Statement of topic

Now, teacher will announce the topic, "Today, I shall teach you about various kinds of noun".

(7) Presentation

Teaching Steps	Teacher's Activity	Student's Activity
Step I: Proper and Common Noun	The teacher will write some sentences on the blackboard, which are as follows: (a) Kolkata is a city. (b) Prachi is a beautiful girl. (c) India is our country. (d) Mohak is a sweet boy. Further, s/he will ask the following questions: (a) What is Kolkata here? (b) Pick out nouns from the sentence (b). (c) What is 'Prachi' in sentence (b)? (d) What is 'India'? (e) Whose name is Mohak in sentence (d)? (f) Pick out nouns from the sentence (d).	 (a) Name of a city. (b) Prachi and girl. (c) Beautiful girl. (d) A country. (e) A particular sweet boy. (f) Mohak and boy.
Generalisation	**Proper Noun:** A proper noun is the name of some particular persons, place or things (as Kolkata, Prachi,	The students will note it down in their notebooks.

	India, Rahul in these sentences). **Common Noun:** A common noun is a name given in common to every person, place or thing of the same class or kind (as city, girl, country, boy in these sentences).	
Step II: Collective Noun	The teacher will write some sentences on the black-board, which are as follows: (a) The herd of cattle is passing. (b) This is a bunch of keys. (c) The French army was defeated at waterloo. (d) The cop dispersed the crowd. Further, s/he will ask the following questions: (a) What does the word 'herd' indicate? (b) What does the word 'bunch' indicate? (c) What does the word 'army' stand for? (d) What does the word 'crowd' stand for?	(a) It indicates the collection of cattle. (b) It indicates the collection of things. (c) It stands for the collection of soldiers. (d) It stands for the collection of persons.
Generalisation	**Collective Noun:** A collective noun is the name of a number (or collection) of persons or things taken together and spoken of as	The students will note down in their notebooks.

	one whole; for example, crowd, mob, team, flock, army, herd, jury, family, parliament, committee, etc.	
Step III: Abstract Noun	The teacher will write some sentences on the blackboard, which are as follows: (a) Sonu is suffering from poor health. (b) The students are reading physics books. (c) Mohan felt a great pain. (d) The class is studying music. Further, s/he will ask the following questions: (a) What does the word 'health' indicate? (b) What is physics? (c) What does the word 'pain' show? (d) What is music?	(a) It indicates a state. (b) Name of science branch. (c) It shows a feeling. (d) Music is an art.
Generalisation	**Abstract Noun:** An Abstract noun is usually the name of a quality, action or state considered apart from the objects to which it belongs. For example, Quality: Bravery, goodness, honesty, kindness, whiteness brightness, etc. Action: Judgement, theft, laughter, movement, hatred, judgement, etc. State: Childhood, boyhood, youth, slavery, sleep, etc.	The students will note down in their notebooks.

(8) Evaluation

- Point out the nouns in the following sentences, and say whether they are common, proper, collective or abstract:

    (a) Always speak the truth.

    (b) Our team is better than theirs.

    (c) We saw a fleet of ships in the harbour.

    (d) Never tell a lie.

    (e) Cleanliness is next to godliness.

    (f) I recognised your voice at once.

- Fill in the blanks with the help of the words given in the brackets:

    (a) _____ is the best policy.   (Abstract Noun)

    (b) _____ was a strong man.   (Proper Noun)

    (c) India is our _____.   (Common Noun)

    (d) We saw a _____ of cattle in the field.   (Collective Noun)

    (e) _____ is wealth.   (Abstract Noun)

(9) Homework

- Make a list of noun of each type from your daily life experiences.

- Describe various kinds of nouns with examples.

LESSON PLAN — 12

Subject: English	**Date:** _____
Topic: Adjective and its kinds	**Duration:** 35 – 40 minutes
	Class: 7th

(1) General Objectives

- To enable the students to understand, write and speak English correctly.
- To develop communication skills of the students.
- To develop the vocabulary and language style.
- To enable them to get knowledge contained in the lesson.
- To inculcate creativity in students.

(2) Specific Objectives

- To enable the students to learn about adjectives and its various kinds.
- To enable the students to use various kinds of adjectives.
- To enable the students to classify the adjectives.

(3) Previous Knowledge

The students must have general familiarities with nouns and pronouns.

(4) Teaching Aids

Blackboard, chalk, duster, pointer, etc.

(5) Introduction

Teacher's Question	Student's Answer
(i) Define noun.	(i) Word used as the name of a person, place or thing.
(ii) Good, now define pronoun.	(ii) Word that takes the place of a noun.
(iii) Alka is a clever girl. (What kind of girl is Alka?)	(iii) Clever.
(iv) Good, tell me what part of speech is clever?	(iv) ....
(v) Do you know about adjective?	(v) ....

(6) Statement of topic

Now, teacher will announce the topic, "Today, I shall teach you about adjectives and its various kinds".

(7) Presentation

Teaching Step	Teacher's Activity	Student's Activity
Step I: Introduce the topic adjective	The teacher will write some sentences on the blackboard, which are as follows: (a) Dinesh is a smart boy. (b) I love that girl. (c) She gave me thousand rupees. (d) There is a more time for preparation. Further, s/he will ask the following questions: (a) What kind of boy is Dinesh? (b) Which word describes the boy Dinesh in sentence (a)? (c) Which word is giving information about 'girl' in sentence (b)? (d) How many rupees she gave me? (e) How much time is there for preparation? (f) Which word describes time?	(a) Dinesh is a smart boy. (b) Smart. (c) The word 'that' is giving information about girl. (d) She gave me 'thousand' rupees. (e) There is a more time for preparation. (f) The word 'more' describes time.
Generalisation	A word or a phrase used with a noun or pronoun to describe or point out a	The students will carefully listen and note down in their notebooks.

	particular person, animal, thing or place which the noun names or to tell the number of quantity is called an adjective. In sentence (a), the adjective lazy is used along with the noun boy as an epithet or attribute. It is therefore said to be used attributively. In sentence (b), the adjective lazy is used along with the verb and forms part of the predicate. It is therefore said to be used predicatively.	
Step II: Kinds of adjectives (Adjectives of Quality or Descriptive Adjectives)	The teacher will write some sentences on the blackboard, which are as follows: (a) Prachi is an innocent girl. (b) Rose is a beautiful flower. (c) The foolish crow tried to swim. (d) Delhi is a large city. Further, s/he will ask the following questions: (a) What kind of girl is Prachi? (b) What kind of flower is rose? (c) What kind of crow tried to swim? (d) What kind of city is Delhi?	(a) Innocent. (b) Beautiful. (c) Foolish. (d) Large.

	(e) What does the word 'large' indicate?	(e) Quality of Delhi.
	(f) What do these words– 'innocent', 'beautiful', 'foolish' and 'large' indicate?	(f) Quality.
Generalisation	An adjective of quality (or descriptive adjectives) shows the kind or quality of a person or thing.	The students will note down in their notebooks.
Step III: Adjective of Quantity	The teacher will write some sentences on the blackboard, which are as follows: (a) We have many exercises. (b) Mohan showed me much patience. (c) We ate some dishes. (d) The whole sum was expanded. Further, s/he will ask the following questions:	
	(a) How much exercises we have?	(a) Many.
	(b) What does the word 'many' indicate?	(b) Quantity.
	(c) How much patience Mohan showed?	(c) Much.
	(d) What does the word 'much' indicate?	(d) Quantity.
	(e) How much dishes did we eat?	(e) Some.
	(f) What does the word 'some' indicate?	(f) Quantity.
	(g) How much sum was expanded?	(g) Whole.

	(h) What does the word 'whole' represent?	(h) Quantity.
Generalisation	An adjective showing the quantity of nouns or pronouns is called an adjective of quantity. An adjective of quantity answers the question: "How much?"	The students will note down in their notebooks.
Step IV: Adjective of Number (or Numeral Adjective)	The teacher will write some sentences on the blackboard, which are as follows: (a) All humans must die. (b) Most girls like dancing. (c) Few cats like cold milk. (d) The hand has five fingers. Further, s/he will ask the following questions:	
	(a) How many humans must die?	(a) All humans.
	(b) How many girls like dancing?	(b) Most girls.
	(c) How many cats like cold milk?	(c) Few cats.
	(d) How many fingers the hand has?	(d) Five fingers.
	(e) What does the word 'five' indicate?	(e) Number.
	(f) What do the word 'All', 'Few', 'Most' and 'Five' indicate?	(f) Number.
Generalisation	An adjective showing the number of nouns or pronouns is called an adjective of number.	The students will note down in their notebooks.

| Step V: Demonstrative Adjective | The teacher will write some sentences on the blackboard, which are as follows:
(a) These grapes are sour.
(b) That girl is beautiful.
(c) This boy is my enemy.
(d) Yonder fort once belonged to Shivaji.
(e) I hate love stories.
Further, s/he will ask the following questions:
(a) Which grapes are sour?
(b) Which girl is beautiful?
(c) Which boy is my enemy?
(d) Which fort once belonged to Shivaji?
(e) What the word 'Yonder' points out?
(f) Which stories I hate? |

(a) These grapes.
(b) That girl.
(c) This boy.
(d) 'Yonder' fort.

(e) Fort.

(f) Love stories. |
| Generalisation | Demonstrative adjective is an adjective that points out which person, object or concept is being referred to; whether it is singular or plural.
(Demonstrative adjective answer the question: Which?)
(It will be noticed that this and that are used with singular nouns; these and those with plural nouns) | The students will note down in their notebooks. |

(8) Evaluation

- Pick out all the adjectives in the following sentences and say which class each of them belongs:
  - (a) Neither party is quite in the right.
  - (b) What time is it?
  - (c) Which pen do you prefer?
  - (d) Nuran won the first prize.
  - (e) There should not be much talk and little work.
  - (f) Good wine needs no bush.
- Fill in the blanks with suitable adjectives.
  - (a) His reading is of a _____ range.
  - (b) The _____ women lived in a wretched hut.
  - (c) Akbar was a _____ king.
  - (d) Everybody loves _____ children.
  - (e) _____ the members were present there.

(9) Homework

- Define adjectives with examples.
- Define the various types of adjectives with proper examples.

LESSON PLAN — 13

Subject: English	Date: _____
Topic: Preposition and its kinds	Duration: 35 – 40 minutes
	Class: 8th

(1) General Objectives

- To enable the students to understand, write and speak English correctly.
- To develop communication skills of the students.
- To develop the vocabulary and language style.
- To enable them to get knowledge contained in the lesson.
- To inculcate creativity in students.

(2) Specific Objectives

- To enable the students to define prepositions and their use in their own words.
- To enable the students to learn about various kinds of preposition.

(3) Previous Knowledge

The students must have general familiarities with different parts of speech, i.e. nouns, pronouns, adjective, verb, adverb, etc.

(4) Teaching Aids

Blackboard, chalk, duster, pointer, etc.

(5) Introduction

Teacher's Question	Student's Answer
(i) What do you know about parts of speech?	(i) The parts of speech are noun, adjective, pronoun, verb, adverb, preposition, conjunction and interjection.
(ii) Good, define noun.	(ii) Word used as the name of a person, place, or thing.
(iii) Define pronoun.	(iii) Word that takes the place of a noun.

(iv) Well, tell me about adjectives.	(iv) A word or a phrase used with a noun or pronoun to describe or point out the person, animal, thing or place which the noun names or to tell the number of quantity.
(v) What do you know about verb?	(v) Word used to express an action or state.
(vi) Good, what do you know about adverb?	(vi) Word used to add something to the meaning of a verb, an adjective or another adverb.
(vii) Do you know about prepositions?	(vii) ....

(6) Statement of topic

Now, teacher will announce the topic, "Today, I shall teach you about prepositions and its various kinds".

(7) Presentation

Teaching Step	Teacher's Activity	Student's Activity
Step I: Meaning of preposition	The teacher will write some sentences on the blackboard, which are as follows: (a) The rat jumped off the table. (b) He is fond of cold–drinks. (c) There is a buffalo in the garden. Further, s/he will ask the following questions: (a) Which parts of speech are in the words 'jumped' and 'table'? (b) Which word is presenting the relationship between verb and noun in sentence(a)?	(a) Jumped: Verb Table: Noun (b) The word 'off'.

	(c) Which parts of speech are in the words 'fond' and 'cold–drinks' in sentence (b)?	(c) Fond: Adjective Cold–drinks: Noun
	(d) What is the function of 'of' in sentence (b)?	(d) Shows relationship between noun and adjective.
	(e) Which parts of speech are in the words buffalo and garden in sentence (c)?	(e) Buffalo: Noun Garden: Noun
	(f) Which word is showing relationship between 'buffalo' and 'garden'?	(f) The word 'in'.
Generalisation	The words off, of, in are here used as prepositions. A preposition is a word placed before a noun or a pronoun to show in what relation the person or thing denoted by it stands in regarding to something else. (The word preposition means 'that which is placed before') It will be noticed that: In sentence (a), the preposition joins a noun to a verb. In sentence (b), the preposition joins a noun to an adjective. In sentence (c), the preposition joins a noun to a verb.	The students will carefully listen and note down in their notebooks.

Step II: Kinds of Prepositions	Prepositions are of five different kinds: (a) Simple prepositions (b) Compound prepositions (c) Double prepositions (d) Participle prepositions (e) Phrase prepositions	The students will note down in their notebooks.
Simple Preposition	Simple prepositions are words like in, on, at, about, over, under, off, of, for, to, etc. For example: (a) She sat on the sofa. (b) He is going to the market. (c) He fell off the ladder. (d) There is some water in the bottle. (e) She is about seven. (f) They sat around the table. (g) The cat was hiding under the bed.	The students will note down in their notebooks.
Compound Preposition	Compound prepositions are words like without, within, inside, outside, into, beneath, below, behind, between, etc. For example: (a) He fell into the river. (b) She sat between her kids. (c) He sat beside her. (d) There is nothing inside the jar. (e) The teacher stood behind the desk. (f) The boy ran across the road.	The students will note down in their notebooks.

Double prepositions	Double prepositions are words like outside of, out of, from behind, from beneath, etc. For example, (a) Suddenly, he emerged from behind the curtain. (b) He walked out of the compound.	The students will note down in their notebooks.
Participle prepositions	Participle prepositions are words like concerning, notwithstanding, pending, considering, etc. For example: (a) There was little chance of success, notwithstanding they decided to go ahead. (b) You did the job well, considering your age and inexperience.	The students will note down in their notebooks.
Phrase prepositions	Phrase prepositions are phrases like because of, by means of, with regard to, on behalf of, instead of, on account of, in opposition to, for the sake of, etc. For example: (a) I am standing here on behalf of my friends and colleagues. (b) The match was cancelled because of the rain. (c) He succeeded by means of perseverance.	The students will note down in their notebooks.

(8) Evaluation

Name the prepositions in the following sentences and tell the word which each governs:

- The lion and the unicorn fought for the crown.
- She sat by the fire and told me a tale.
- A fair little girl sat under a tree.
- Humpty Dumpty sat on a wall.
- I can never return with my poor dog Tray.
- I tried to reason him out of his fears.

(9) Homework

- Define preposition with examples.
- Define the various types of prepositions with proper examples.

LESSON PLAN — 14

Subject: English	Date: _____
Topic: Future Tense	Duration: 35 – 40 minutes
	Class: 9th

(1) General Objectives

- To enable the students to understand, write and speak English correctly.
- To develop communication skills of the students.
- To develop the vocabulary and language style.
- To enable them to get knowledge contained in the lesson.
- To inculcate creativity in students.

(2) Specific Objectives

- To enable the students to learn about the Future Tense.
- To enable them to use the rule of future tense.

(3) Previous Knowledge

The students must have general familiarities with different parts of speech, present and past tenses and can understand simple English.

(4) Teaching Aids

Blackboard, chalk, duster, pointer, etc.

(5) Introduction

Teacher's Question	Student's Answer
(i) What do you know about parts of speech?	(i) The parts of speech are noun, adjective, pronoun, verb, adverb, preposition, conjunction and interjection.
(ii) Good, what do you know about tenses?	(ii) The time of a verb's action or state of being, such as present or past.
(iii) Tell the types of tenses.	(iii) Present tense, past tense and future tense.

(iv) Good, tell me about subject and object in tense.	(iv) The part that names the person or thing we are speaking about is subject. The word or group of words, functioning as a noun or a pronoun, that is influenced by a verb or a preposition is object.
(v) Do you know about the rules of future tense?	(v) ....

(6) Statement of topic

Now, teacher will announce the topic, "Today, I shall teach you about future tense and its rules".

(7) Presentation

Teaching Step	Teacher's Activity	Student's Activity
Simple Future Tense	Teacher will tell that the simple future tense is used to talk about things, which we cannot control. It expresses the future as a fact. The rule for Simple Future tense is as follows: Sub + will/shall + Ist form of verb + Obj For Example: (a) We will know our exam results in March. (b) I shall answer the letter tonight.	The students will carefully listen and note down in their notebooks.
Future Continuous Tense	Teacher will tell that we use the future continuous tense to talk about actions, which will be in progress at a time in the future. The rule for Future Continuous tense is as follows: Sub + will/shall + be + verb + ing + Obj For Example: (a) I will be staying here till Friday.	The students will carefully listen and note down in their notebooks.

	(b) The fight show will be coming soon. (c) We shall be going to Shimla tomorrow.	
Future Perfect Tense	Teacher will tell that the future perfect tense is used to talk about actions that will be in completed by a certain future time. The rule for Future Perfect tense is as follows: Sub + will/shall + have + IIIrd form of verb + Obj For Example: (a) We will have returned home by five o'clock. (b) I shall have written my exercise tomorrow. (c) He will have left before you go to see him.	The students will carefully listen and note down in their notebooks.
Future Perfect Continuous	Teacher will tell that the future perfect continuous tense is used for actions, which will be in progress over a period of time that will end in the future. The rule for Future Perfect Continuous tense is as follows: Sub + will/shall + have + been + verb + ing + Since/for + Obj **Note**: *For* is used when specifying the amount of time (how long) and can also be used in all tenses. *Since* is used when specifying the starting point of the work and can also be used in perfect tenses only.	The students will carefully listen and note down in their notebooks.

| | For Example:
(a) I'll have been teaching for ten years next August.
(b) By next September, we shall have been living here for four years.
(c) They will have been playing since ten o'clock. | |

(8) Evaluation

Choose the correct or more suitable forms of the verbs to fill in the blanks.

- I think India _____ win the match. (will, shall)
- This time tomorrow, I _____ sitting on the beach in Singapore. (will, will be, will have been)
- Children_____ fly kite in the sky. (will, will be)
- We _____ buy some books. (will, shall)
- They _____ learning for two years. (will have been, will have, will be)

(9) Homework

Learn the rules of all the future tenses and write some sentences in your notebooks.

LESSON PLAN — 15

Subject: English	**Date:** _____
Topic: Active Voice and Passive Voice	**Duration:** 35 – 40 minutes
	Class: 10th

(1) General Objectives

- To enable the students to understand, write and speak English correctly.
- To develop communication skill of the students.
- To develop the vocabulary and language style.
- To enable them to get knowledge contained in the lesson.
- To inculcate creativity in students.

(2) Specific Objectives

- To enable the students to learn about active voice and passive voice.
- To enable them to use active voice and passive voice.

(3) Previous Knowledge

The students must have general familiarities with different parts of speech, tenses and can understand simple English.

(4) Teaching Aids

Blackboard, chalk, duster, pointer, etc.

(5) Introduction

Teacher's Question	Student's Answer
(i) What do you know about parts of speech?	(i) The parts of speech are Noun, Adjective, Pronoun, Verb, Adverb, Preposition, Conjunction and Interjection.
(ii) Good, define noun.	(ii) Word used as the name of a person, place or thing.
(iii) Define pronoun.	(iii) Word that takes the place of a noun.

(iv) What do you know about verb?	(iv) Word used to express an action or state.
(v) What do you know about tenses?	(v) The time of a verb's action or state of being, such as present or past.
(vi) Tell the types of tenses.	(vi) Present tense, past tense and future tense.
(vii) In which process, the places of subject and object are interchanged?	(vii) ....
(viii) Do you know about active or passive voice?	(viii) ....

(6) Statement of topic

Now, teacher will announce the topic, "Today, I shall teach you about active voice and passive voice and how to change active voice into passive voice".

(7) Presentation

Teaching Step	Teacher's Activity	Student's Activity
Compare	(a) Prachi helps Priya. (b) Priya is helped by Prachi. After writing the above sentences on the blackboard, the teacher will tell all the students that these two sentences express the same meaning. But in sentence (a), the form of the verb shows that the person denoted by the subject does something. Prachi (the person denoted by the subject) does something. The verb helps is said to be in the active voice.	The students will listen attentively and note down in their notebooks.

	In sentence (b), the form of the verb shows that something is done to the person denoted by the subject. Something is done to Priya (the person denoted by the subject.) The verb helped is said to be in the passive voice.	
Active Voice	A verb is used in the active voice when its form shows (as in sentence a) that the person or thing denoted by the subject does something or, in other words, is the doer of the action.	The students will listen attentively and note down in their notebooks.
Passive Voice	A verb is the passive voice when its form shows (as in sentence b) that something is done to the person or thing denoted by the subject.	The students will listen attentively and note down in their notebooks.
Change of Active Voice into Passive Voice	*Active Voice* / *Passive Voice* table below	The students will listen attentively and note down in their notebooks.

Active Voice	Passive Voice
(a) Mohit hates Vikas.	(a) Vikas is hated by Mohit.
(b) Who did this?	(b) By whom was this done?
(c) Naina will finish the chocolate.	(c) The chocolate will be finished by Naina.
(d) The peon opened the gate.	(d) The gate was opened by the peon.

After drawing the above table on the blackboard, the teacher will tell all the students to note the change from the active voice to the passive voice in sentences given in the table.

	It will be noticed that when the verb is changed from the active voice to the passive voice, the object of the verb in the active voice becomes the subject of the verb in the passive voice. (Thus in sentence 'a', Vikas, who is the object of 'hates' in the active voice, becomes the subject of 'is hated' in the passive voice.)	
Generalisation	While changing active voice into passive voice, in passive voice the helping verb is used after the subject according to the tense used in active voice and the subject of the passive voice. Study the following table:	The students will listen attentively and note down in their notebooks.

Tense	Active Voice	Passive Voice
Simple Present	take takes	am taken is taken are taken
Present continuous	am taking is taking are taking	am being taken is being taken are being taken
Present perfect	has taken have taken	has been taken have been taken
Simple past	took	was taken were taken
Past continuous	was taking were taking	was being taken were being taken
Past perfect	had taken	had been taken
Simple Future	will take shall take	will be taken shall be taken
can/may/must, etc.+ base	can take must take	can be taken must be taken

Use of IIIrd Form of Verb	(a) Active Voice: Nidhi saves the bird. Passive Voice: The bird is saved by Nidhi. (b) Active Voice: Naseem helps Vikas. Passive Voice: Vikas was helped by Naseem. After writing the above sentences on the blackboard, the teacher will ask the following questions: (a) Which verbs are used in active voice? (b) Which form of verb is used in active voice (a)? (c) Which form of verb is used in active voice (b)? (d) Which main verbs are used in passive voice? (e) Which form of verb is used in passive voice?	 (a) 'Save' and 'help'. (b) Ist form of verb according to Present Indefinite tense. (c) IInd form of verb according to Past Indefinite tense. (d) 'Saved' and 'helped'. (e) The IIIrd form of verb is used in passive voice.
Generalisation	Teacher will tell that when we convert a sentence from active voice to passive voice, the IIIrd form of verb is used with helping verb.	The students will listen attentively and note down in their notebooks.
Use of Pre-position 'By'	*Active Voice:* Mr. Vikas teaches us grammar. *Passive Voice:* Grammar is taught to us by Mr. Vikas. After writing the above sentences	

	on the blackboard, the teacher will ask the following questions: (a) Which is the extra word used just before object in passive voice? (b) Which part of speech is 'by'? (c) Where is this preposition 'by' put in passive voice?				(a) By. (b) Preposition. (c) It is put or used just before the object.		
Generalisation	Teacher will tell that while changing active voice into passive voice before the object the preposition 'by' is used.				The students will listen attentively and note down in their notebooks.		
Structure of Passive Voice	Rule: Subject + Helping Verb + IIIrd form of Main Verb + By + Object.						

S.No.	Voice	Subject	Helping Verb	Main Verb	Pre-position	Object
1.	A.V. P.V.	Sohan Lie	– is	hates hated	– by	lie. Sohan.
2.	A.V. P.V.	Horse Child	– was	frighte ned frighte ned	– by	child. horse.
3.	A.V. P.V.	Somebody My pen	– was	stole stolen	– by	my pen. Some-body.

(8) Evaluation

- Name the verbs in the following sentences, and tell whether they are in the active voice or in the passive voice.

  (a) The captive was bound to a tree.

  (b) The ship was burned.

  (c) He is loved by all.

  (d) The dog chased the sheep.

  (e) The money was lost.

  (f) The letter has just been posted.

- Turn the following sentences from the active voice to the passive voice:

  (a) Sonu opened the door.

  (b) He beats his brother.

  (c) My father will write a letter.

  (d) I have sold my car.

  (e) A policeman caught the thief.

  (f) We prohibit smoking.

(9) Homework

- Define active and passive voice.

- Explain the different rules of changing active voice into passive voice.

Composition

LESSON PLAN — 16

Subject: English	**Date:** _____
Topic: "Leave Application"	**Duration:** 35 – 40 minutes
	Class: 8th

(1) General Objectives

- To enable the students to understand, write and speak English correctly.
- To develop communication skills and logical thinking of the students.
- To develop in them a habit of clear and logical presentation of facts.
- To enable them to get knowledge contained in the lesson.
- To inculcate creativity in students.

(2) Specific Objectives

- To enable the students to compose an application to the principal for leave.
- To familiarise the students with different parts of the application.
- To enable the students to use appropriate vocabulary and structure while composing an application.

(3) Previous Knowledge

The students must have general familiarities with meaning of the word 'application' and also with letter writing.

(4) Teaching Aids

Blackboard, chalk, duster, pointer, etc.

(5) Introduction

Teacher's Question	Student's Answer
(i) How many types of letters are there? Name them.	(i) There are two types of letter, i.e. formal and informal letters.

(ii) Do you know what the name of leave taking official letter is?	(ii) Yes, application.
(iii) Good, do you know what the meaning of an application is?	(iii) Application may refer to a verbal or written request.
(iv) Well, how to write an application for leave to the principal?	(iv) ....

(6) Statement of topic

Now, teacher will announce the topic, "Today, I shall teach you about how to write an application for leave to the principal".

(7) Presentation

Teaching Step	Teacher's Activity	Student's Activity
Parts of an Application	The teacher will write a model of application for leave to the principal on blackboard, which is as follows: To The Principal G.P.H. School New Delhi. Date Subject: Leave Application *Salutation:* Respected Sir/Mam *Body of Letter or Content:* I beg to say that	Students will note it down in their notebooks.

	.... *Subscription* Thanking you Yours Obediently Further, she will tell them the following directions: (a) The heading consists of the address of the school. (b)Then, write date and subject of the application (c) The courteous Greeting or Salutation. (d) The Communication or Message: The body of the letter. (e) The Subscription.	
Content of the application	The teacher will write an application for leave to the principal on black-board, which is as follows: To The Principal G.P.H. School New Delhi. x/x/x	

	Subject: Leave Application	
	Respected Sir,	
	I beg to say that I am Vikas Sahni, student of class Xth in your school, suffering from severe fever. Therefore, I cannot attend the school. Kindly grant me leave for two days.	
	Thanking you Yours obediently Vikas Sahni Xth–A	
	Further, she will ask the following questions:	
	(a) How can we start the body of an application?	(a) We can start writing by (a) "I beg to say that" or "With due respect I beg to say that".
	(b) How do you further continue the application?	(b) After it, we shall put the reason for leave as "I am suffering from severe fever" or "I am suffering from headache" or "I have an important piece of work at home," etc.
	(c) What will you write after giving an appropriate reason?	(c) We shall mention it in the subscription by writing "Thanking you."

(8) Evaluation

Write an application to the principal for fee–concession according to the same guidelines.

(9) Homework

Suppose, you want leave for two days to attend a marriage at Varanasi. Write an application to the principal of the school for the same.

LESSON PLAN — 17

Subject: English	Date: _____
Topic: Essay writing (Population Growth)	Duration: 35 – 40 minutes
	Class: 9th

(1) General Objectives

- To enable the students to understand, write and speak English correctly.
- To develop communication skills and logical thinking of the students.
- To develop in them a habit of clear and logical presentation of facts.
- To enable them to get knowledge contained in the lesson.
- To inculcate creativity in students.

(2) Specific Objectives

- To enable the students to know about population growth.
- To enable the students to understand the cause of population growth.
- To enable the students to reason out the disadvantages of population growth.
- To familiarise the students with different styles of writing composition.
- To enable the students to use appropriate vocabulary and structure while composing an essay.

(3) Previous Knowledge

The students must have at least general awareness with population growth.

(4) Teaching Aids

Blackboard, chalk, duster, pointer, etc.

(5) Introduction

Teacher's Question	Student's Answer
(i) Where do you live?	(i) Noida.
(ii) What kind of place is it?	(ii) Industrial area.

(iii) Why are small towns and villages more comfortable to live in?	(iii) Since there are less number of people living there, hence, small towns and villages more comfortable to live in.
(iv) Do you know the reasons of population growth?	(iv) ....
(v) Can you write an essay on it?	(v) ....

(6) Statement of topic

Now, teacher will announce the topic, "Today, we shall develop a composition/essay on "population growth".

(7) Presentation

Teaching Step	Teacher's Activity	Student's Activity
Oral development of composition	The teacher will start oral development composition and speak sentences by pointing towards the various aspects of the essay. He will also write the outline of the essay on the blackboard side by side. The outline on the blackboard is as follows: One major problem that the world faces today is the rapid growth of population often referred to as population explosion. Until 800 AD, the world population remained below 200 million. Since then it has risen dramatically. The rise has been the greatest in 20th century. The population has risen to about 6 billion, i.e. around 3 times as large as it	The students will listen carefully and write the outline in their notebooks.

	was in 1960. Experts predict that by 2020 there will be 10 billion people. This will cause problems of hunger, over-crowding and environmental pollution.	
Causes	Teacher will tell about the causes behind the over population and write on the blackboard side by side. The outline on the blackboard is as follows: High growth rate, decline in death rate, improved medical facilities and public health services are the primary causes of rapid population growth. Rapid means of transport and communication have facilitated rapid movement of food–grains from surplus areas to deficit areas. People now don't die due to epidemics, drought or famine. Decrease in infant mortality is also one of the causes of increasing population.	The students will listen attentively and note down in their notebooks.
Harmful effects of rapid population growth	Teacher will tell about the harmful effects of rapid population on society and write on the blackboard side by side. The outline on the blackboard is as follows:	The students will listen attentively and note down in their notebooks.

	Food problems: It is not always possible to increase the output of food to feed new mouths. Land is limited, hence, increase in population decreases per capita land area for agricultural operations. *Increase in unemployment:* It has become difficult to provide employment opportunities to the vast army of unemployed. *Difficulty in capital formation:* Increase in population has resulted in decrease of savings and capital formation. *Bleak future of Five–Year Plans:* Rapid growth in population is associated with drought, famine, war, or political disturbances. As a result, plans are never successful. Set targets are never achieved. The national, as well as per capita income does not increase by the same rate as planned and envisaged.	
Conclusion	The teacher will tell about a conclusion behind over the population growth and write on the blackboard side by side. The outline on the	The students will listen attentively and note down in their notebooks.

	blackboard is as follows: With a population of over one billion, India is the 2nd most populous country in the world (China is the first). The population today is $2\frac{1}{2}$ times as large as it was in 1950. The government is taking measures to check the population growth. It is rising by 2.9 per cent per year. Recent advances in farming have made the country productive enough to feed the present population. According to Julia Simon although population growth means more months to feed, there will be more hands to work and more brains to think.	

(8) Evaluation

The students will be asked to write the composition themselves in the class.

(9) Homework

Write a short essay on increase in unemployment due to over population.

Why Students Choose GPH Books?

- Syllabus covered as prescribed by Universities/Boards/Institutions.

- Easily understandable language and format that help students prepare for exam in short period of time.

- Published with exam-oriented approach, hence prepared in question-answer format which provides students the instant understanding of a correct answer.

- Maximum solved previous year question papers included which help students to understand unique examination structure and equip them better for exam.

- Both semesters' question papers (June-December) are included with solutions.

- Instant updation of data as and when any change occurs.

- Use of recycled paper.

- Handy books and reasonable prices.

- For every book sold, we contribute for society/institution/NGOs/underprivileged

Translation

LESSON PLAN — 18

Subject: English	**Date:** _____
Topic: Present Perfect Tense	**Duration:** 35 – 40 minutes
	Class: 6th

(1) General Objectives

- To enable the students to understand, write and speak English correctly.
- To develop communication skills and logical thinking of the students.
- To develop in them a habit of clear and logical presentation of facts.
- To enable them to get knowledge contained in the lesson.
- To enable them to translate from English to mother tongue and mother tongue to English.

(2) Specific Objectives

- To enable the students to translate sentences of Present Perfect tense into English.
- To enable the students in developing the practice of translating the sentences of Present Perfect tense.
- To expose the students to use of Present Perfect tense.

(3) Previous Knowledge

The students have working knowledge of mother tongue Hindi and can recognise the sentences of Present Perfect tense in Hindi. They have already studied how to translate the sentences of Present Indefinite and Present Continuous tense into English.

(4) Teaching Aids

Blackboard, chalk, duster, pointer, etc.

(5) Introduction

Teacher's Question	Student's Answer
(i) The teacher will ask the students to translate the following sentences: (a) मैं खाना खाता हूँ। (b) राहुल किताब पढ़ता है। (c) बच्चे मैदान में क्रिकेट खेल रहे हैं। (d) नसीम सो रहा है। (e) निखिल फुटबॉल खेल रहा है।	(a) I eat food. (b) Rahul reads book. (c) Children are playing cricket in garden. (d) Naseem is sleeping. (e) Nikhil is playing football.
(ii) The teacher will ask about the type of tense used in these sentences.	(ii) Present Indefinite or Present Continuous tense.
(iii) Translate the following sentences: (a) तनिक्षा जूस पी चुकी है। (b) सोनू मंदिर जा चुका है।	(iii) (a) .... (b) ....
(iv) Which tense is used in these sentences?	(iv) ....

(6) Statement of topic

Now, teacher will announce the topic, "Today, we shall learn and understand how to translate the Hindi sentences of Present Perfect tense into English".

(7) Presentation

Teaching Steps	Teacher's Activity	Student's Activity
Step I: Affirmative and Negative Sentences	The teacher will present the following sentences of Hindi with their translation on a blackboard, which are as follows: (a) सोहन जा चुका है। Sohan has gone. (b) बच्चे दूध पी चुके हैं। Children have drunk milk. (c) हम बाजार से आ चुके हैं। We have come from market. (d) मैं नहीं सोया हूँ। I have not slept.	The students will listen carefully and write the outline in their notebooks.

	Further, she will ask the following questions: (a) What are Sohan, Children, We and I in all these sentences? (b) What is used after subject of a sentence? (c) Which helping verb is used in these sentences? (d) Which form of main verb is used? (e) What is used between helping and main verb in sentence (d)? (f) Why is the word 'not' is used here?	(a) Subjects. (b) Helping verb (c) has/have (d) 3rd form of main verb (e) The word 'not.' (f) Because it is a negative sentence.
Generalisation	While translating Hindi sentences of Present Perfect tense, helping verb is used according to the number of subject and it is followed by IIIrd form of verb and in 'Negative Sentences' the word 'not' comes between helping verb and main verb. The rule for affirmative and negative sentences are as follows: (a) Affirmative Sentence: Subject + has/have + IIIrd form of verb + object. (b) Negative Sentence: Subject + has/have + not + IIIrd form of verb + object. To analyse the sentences of Present Perfect tense, the	The students will listen attentively and note down in their notebooks.

	teacher will present the following chart.					
	S.No.	Subject	Helping verb	Not	Main verb	Object
	(a) Affirmative Sentences					
	(i)	I	have	–	known	him.
	(ii)	Ram	has	–	eaten	pasta.
	(iii)	They	have	–	finished	the work.
	(b) Negative Sentences					
	(i)	He	has	not	read	the books.
	(ii)	Children	have	not	done	their homework.
	(iii)	Vikas	has	not	left	the station.

Step II: Interrogative Sentence	The teacher will present the following sentences of Hindi with their translation on a black-board, which are as follows: (a) क्या सोनू खाना खा चुका है? Has Sonu eaten food? (b) क्या भारती सो चुकी है? Has Bharti slept? (c) क्या तुम किताब पढ़ चुके हो? Have you read a book? (d) क्या तुम मिठाई खा चुके हो? Have you eaten sweets? Further, she will ask the following questions: (i) Which is the first word in sentence (a)? (ii) What is kept after has/have? (iii) What is used after the subject? (iv) Which mark is used after the object?	(i) 'has/have' the helping verb is the first word. (ii) Subject. (iii) IIIrd form of verb. (iv) The interrogation mark.
Generalisation	While translating Hindi sentences of Interrogative form in Present Perfect Tense, helping verb is used before subject and its sequence will be:	The students will listen attentively and note down in their notebooks.

S.No.	Helping Verb	Subject	IIIrd form of Main Verb	Object
(a)	Has	Bhanu	written	a letter?
(b)	Have	children	eaten	mangoes?
(c)	Have	they	done	their work?

Helping verb + Subject + IIIrd form of Main Verb + Object?
Now, the teacher will present the following chart to analyse the Present Perfect tense:

(8) Evaluation

Translate the following sentences:

- क्या मैं गाना गा चुका हूँ?
- नीतू स्कूल से आ चुकी है।
- मैं अपना गृहकार्य कर चुका हूँ।
- क्या राम और श्याम सो चुके हैं?
- क्या तुम कपड़े धो चुके हो?

(9) Homework

Fill the gaps with correct Present Perfect form of verb given in brackets:

- Ram .... out. (go)
- You .... G.P.H. books. (read)
- I .... my finger. (cut)
- Dinesh .... his M.Com. (complete)
- They .... the bridge. (build)

LESSON PLAN — 19

Subject: English	**Date:** _____
Topic: Past Continuous Tense	**Duration:** 35 – 40 minutes
	Class: 7th

(1) General Objectives

- To enable the students to understand, write and speak English correctly.
- To develop communication skills and logical thinking of the students.
- To develop in them a habit of clear and logical presentation of facts.
- To enable them to get knowledge contained in the lesson.
- To enable them to translate from English to mother tongue and mother tongue to English.

(2) Specific Objectives

- To enable the students to translate sentences of Past Continuous tense into English.
- To enable the students in developing the practice of translating the sentence of Past Continuous tense.
- To expose the students to use of Past Continuous tense.

(3) Previous Knowledge

The students have working knowledge of mother tongue Hindi and can recognise the sentences of Past Continuous tense in Hindi. They have already studied how to translate the sentences of Present tense and Past Indefinite tense into English.

(4) Teaching Aids

Blackboard, chalk, duster, pointer, etc.

(5) Introduction

Teacher's Question	Student's Answer
(i) The teacher will ask the students to translate the following sentences:	
(a) मैं खाना खाता हूँ।	(a) I eat food

(b) राहुल किताब पढ़ता है।	(b) Rahul reads book.
(c) बच्चे मैदान में क्रिकेट खेल रहे हैं।	(c) Children are playing cricket in garden.
(d) नसीम सो रहा है।	(d) Nadeem is sleeping.
(e) मैंने कानपुर में इंग्लिश सीखी है।	(e) I learnt English in Kanpur.
(ii) The teacher will ask about the kind of tense used in these sentences.	(ii) Present Indefinite, Present Continuous or Past Indefinite tense.
(iii) Translate the following sentences: (a) मैं खाना खा रहा था। (b) सोनू मंदिर जा रहा था।	(iii) (a) .... (b).....................................
(iv) Which tense is used in these sentences?	(iv) ....

(6) Statement of topic

Now, teacher will announce the topic, "Today, we shall learn and understand how to translate the Hindi sentences of Past Continuous tense into English".

(7) Presentation

Teaching Step	Teacher's Activity	Student's Activity
Step I: Affirmative and Negative Sentences	The teacher will present the following sentences of Hindi with their translation on blackboard, which are as follows: (a) हम किताब पढ़ रहे थे। We were reading books. (b) राधा गाना गा रही थी। Radha was singing a song. (c) हम बाजार से आ रहे थे। We were coming from market.	The students will listen carefully and write the outline in their notebooks.

	(d) मैं सो नहीं रहा था।	
	I was not sleeping.	
	Further, she will ask the following questions:	
	(a) What are We, Radha and I in all these sentences?	(a) They all are subjects.
	(b) What is used after subject of the sentence?	(b) Helping verb
	(c) Which helping verb is used in these sentences?	(c) was/were
	(d) Which form of main verb is used?	(d) Ist form of verb with ing.
	(e) What is used between helping and main verbs in sentence (d)?	(e) The word 'not' is used here.
	(f) Why is the word 'not' is used here?	(f) Because it is a negative sentence.
Generalisation	While translating Hindi sentences of Past Continuous Tense, helping verb is used according to the number of subject and is followed by Ist form of verb with ing and in 'Negative Sentences' the word 'not' comes between helping verb and main verb. The rules of affirmative and negative sentences are as follows: (a) Affirmative Sentence: Subject + was/were + Ist form of verb with ing + Object. (b) Negative Sentence: Subject + was/were + not + Ist form of verb with ing + Object.	The students will listen attentively and note down in their notebooks.

| | To analyse the Past Continuous tense, the teacher will present the following chart. | |

S.No.	Subject	Helping verb	Not	Main verb	Object
(a) Affirmative Sentences					
(i)	He	was	–	knowing	him.
(ii)	Ram	was	–	driving	the bus.
(iii)	They	were	–	finished	the lunch.
(b) Negative Sentences					
(i)	They	were	not	eating	the food.
(ii)	Children	were	not	doing	their homework.
(iii)	Vikas	was	not	going	to Shimla .

Step II: Interrogative Sentence	The teacher will present some sentences of Hindi with their translation on blackboard, which are as follows:	
	(a) क्या दिल्ली में बारिश हो रही थी?	
	Was it raining in Delhi?	
	(b) क्या पूरन गाने सुन रहा था?	
	Was Puran listening songs?	
	(c) क्या तुम्हारी कल परीक्षा थी?	
	Were your exams tomorrow?	
	(d) क्या सोनू मिठाई खा रहा था?	
	Was Sonu eating sweets?	
	Further, she will ask the following questions:	
	(i) Which is the first word of a Past Continuous Interrogative sentence?	(i) Was/were.
	(ii) What is kept after was/were?	(ii) Subject.
	(iii) What is used after the subject?	(iii) Ist form of verb with ing.

	(iv) Which mark is used after the object?	(iv) The interrogation mark.
Generalisation	While translating Hindi sentences of Interrogative form in Past Continuous tense, helping verb is used before subject and its sequence will be: Helping verb + Subject + Ist form of Main Verb with ing + Object. To analyse the Past Continuous tense, the teacher will present the following chart:	The students will listen attentively and note down in their notebooks.

S.No.	Helping Verb	Subject	Main Verb	Object
(a)	Was	Bhanu	writing	a letter?
(b)	Were	children	eating	grapes?
(c)	Were	they	doing	their homework?

(8) Evaluation

Translate the following sentences:

- क्या राम खाना खा रहा था?
- नीतू बाजार से आ रही थी।
- मैं अपना गृहकार्य कर रहा था।

(9) Homework

Fill the correct Past Continuous form of verb in gaps with the help of words given in brackets:

- Ram _____ out. (go)
- You _____ G.P.H. books. (read)
- I _____ my finger. (cut)
- Dinesh _____ his M.Com. (complete)
- They _____ the bridge. (build)

✍ ✍ ✍

Gullybaba Kids

> **Focus**   > **Fitness**   > **Respect**

Want to know?

> How to protect kids from screen addiction, junk food, bad habits?

> What games are best for kids' mind development?

> How to make child a responsible citizen?

Like, Comment and Subscribe our Channel

▶ **YouTube**
/gullybabakids

 SUBSCRIBE

4 Microteaching

● ● ●

The quality of education that is provided to our children depends on the quality of our teachers. The quality of teachers, in turn, definitely depends on the way in which they had received training through teacher's training institutions. The question that immediately arises now is about the teacher education programme. Hence, we must take a peep into this programme. The need of planning is essential. If our teachers are going to shape the destiny of our country, teacher education has to assume a great responsibility and has to take recourse to some innovative and effective technique of training teachers. It was believed that just as the director brings the skill of giving life and form to a movie, so the teacher brings to the teaching–learning situation the skill with which s/he is able to control and use his/her teaching exercise and thus influence the other variables of the situation. This skill does not automatically come to the teacher with a certificate or diploma or a teaching contract. Rather, it is a skill developed through the awareness of the interacting elements in a teaching–learning situation, planning strategies for teaching based on this awareness, through the setting of sound objectives, assessing the results and modifying these objectives in terms of assessment. In India, the education system made for the traditional teacher education programme consisted of two major parts:

- Theoretical Course, and
- Practice teaching.

The theoretical course, which covers philosophical, historical, sociological and psychological foundation of education and teaching methodology, is mainly verbal, abstract and vague. Consequently, it affects cognitive and attitudinal rather than behavioural changes in teachers. With regard to practice teaching, it is assumed that during this period, the pupil teacher will develop proficiency in basic teaching skills and classroom management. In actual practice, however, the programme of student teaching tends to him theoretical and lacks the objective feedback on performance, essential to both motivating and directing behavioural modifications. Hence, improvements were felt to the required not only in the theoretical aspect of the teacher–education curriculum, but also in the application of teaching skills.

Definition of Microteaching

Microteaching is a procedure in which a pupil teacher practice teaching with a reduced number of pupils in a reduced period of time with emphasis on a narrow and specific teaching skill. Thus, microteaching is a scaled–down encounter in class size and class time. It is, therefore a skill based approach to teacher training. Microteaching is a technique of presenting a small portion of the lesson for detailed study and pinpointed guidance by taking a microscopic view. Reducing the number of students in the class, the duration of the lesson, the portion of the content and the number of skills to be practiced minimises the complexities of the usual classroom teaching.

Thus, microteaching is a training technique, which requires pupil teachers to teach a single concept, using specified teaching skills to a small number of pupils in a short duration of time. Microteaching is a training technique and the idea underlying this technique is that the teaching act consists of different skills. Each skill can be developed separately through training. The basic contention is that, more the number of skills in which a person is trained, the more efficient s/he will be as a teacher.

Accordingly, this technique is mainly for developing certain skills of teaching procedure, which contains the following steps:
- Modeling the skill.
- Planning a micro lesson.

- The teaching session.
- The critique session.
- The re–planning session.
- The re–teach session.
- The re–critique session.

(1) Modeling the skill

It is essential to orient the trainees in the teaching skill to be practiced. This may be done though stating the psychological base and rationale of the skill and then demonstrating the said skill. This step is called Modeling. Models are of two types:

- **Perceptual Model:** Perceptual model is one, which is presented by way of demonstration and is visually perceived by the trainee.

- **Conceptual Model:** The conceptual model is usually presented in the form of written material and is conceptualised by trainees.

The microteaching technique usually uses the perceptual model, which enables the trainees of focus their attention on the skill to be practiced and to perceive the pinpointed behaviour.

(2) Planning a micro lesson

It is necessary to select an appropriate content, which yields maximum scope for practicing the skill. A lesson of a short duration, usually of 5 to 7 minutes, is then planned in consultation with the supervisor. With these two steps, namely, modeling and lesson planning, the stage is set for safe practice teaching.

(3) The teaching session

The plan of the lesson is now executed in the presence of the supervisor and/or peer trainees. The performance of a micro teacher is observed in relation to the skills to be acquired and is recorded. An evaluation sheet tape recorder, video tapes all of these or either of these evaluation tools is used for this purpose.

(4) The critique session

The students leave the class and the supervisor and/or the peer group discusses the micro teacher's performance. Trainees' concrete and pinpointed feedback is then given in 5 to 7 minutes for the specific improvement. The evaluation tools (videotape, etc.) give a rare opportunity to the micro teacher to view his/her performance objectively. They hardly give him/her an opportunity to put forth self–defence. This is a strong point of the microteaching technique.

(5) The re–planning session

The micro teacher recognises this each teaching plan on the basis of the feedback offered in the critique session. Usually, 5 to 7 minutes are allotted to this.

(6) The re–teaching session

This step provides the micro teacher an opportunity to teach the same unit. The re–planning session is followed by the re–teaching session, which runs for 5 to 7 minutes. The same unit is taught to another batch of 5 to 7 pupils. The supervisor and/or the peer trainee observer evaluate the performance of the micro teacher with the evaluation tools. This step provides the micro teacher an opportunity to teach the same unit without considering time lag.

(7) The re–critique session

The same procedure is adopted as mentioned in the critique session. The micro teacher again gets the feedback and knows the extent of his/her improvement. If handled properly, this step has the potential to motivate the micro teacher to improve his/her performance.

(8) The Seven Steps in Microteaching

The microteaching has seven important steps without which we cannot complete the process. These steps are as follows:

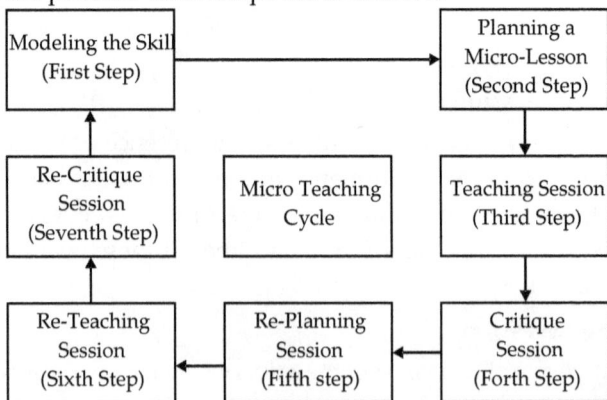

Fig. 4.1

Planning Session, Teaching Session, Critique Session, Re–Planning Session, Re–Teaching Session and Re–Critique Session form one complete cycle of microteaching procedure. This cycle may be repeated according to the necessity of improvement. The entire procedure for a micro–lesson then runs as follows:

First of all, there is a theoretical discussion on a particular skill to be practiced. Its components are defined in precise terms. This is followed by demonstration and modeling. The student teachers observe the particular skill. After this, a suitable unit is chosen and the student teacher prepares a lesson plan and gets ready for a micro–lesson. The lesson is taught and criticised by the peer group. As per criticism/feedback, the student teacher plans his/her lesson again and it goes on.

Microteaching is thus mainly concerned with acquiring the teaching skills. It is thus the planned interaction between the teacher and the taught. Now, it is not possible to go to schools and practice this skill, as the principals of the schools will never like the idea of allowing only 5 to 7 pupils at a time. This will disturb their schedule too. So, to overcome this problem, the student teachers are asked to give lessons to their own peer group. This is called "Simulation". Let us therefore try to understand what simulation is!

Positive Aspects of Microteaching

- There comes a major awareness to pupil teachers with regard to professional training.
- There is more scope for practice in teaching skills according to the student's potential.
- It develops confidence by having the practice of skills in microteaching under simulated conditions.
- It creates more general teaching competence among the pupil–teachers.
- It allows for different strategies for supervisory feedback.
- Microteaching helps to identify categories in which additional research is needed.

- Microteaching helps in improving the methods of criticising student's performance.
- It determines the length of training time required to master certain skills.
- Microteaching helps in improving the ways of analysing pupil learning.
- Microteaching focuses attention on teacher behaviour.
- It offers opportunity to practice a real lesson without the complexities of a normal classroom (great advantage of working under simulated conditions).
- If offers several sources of immediate feedback.
- One skill is learnt at a time.
- It equips the beginner with an array of teaching skills before s/he faces the real classroom situation.
- Evaluation procedure of a micro–lesson is more precise, objective and acceptable.
- Major steps of a micro lesson are towards individualising the training of teachers.
- It helps in the development of self–confidence.
- It helps in being acquainted with classroom manners to a certain extent.
- It helps the trainees to develop the skill of blackboard writing.
- It is helpful in improving his/her own teaching.

Practicing Skills of Questioning in Microteaching

The skill of asking questions in the classroom teaching is very important. By asking questions again and again, the teacher makes the pupils more thoughtful. S/he enables them to understand and subjects deeply. Questions are those, which help the pupils to think in depth about the various aspects of the problem. The teacher can use the questions in the following situations:

(1) Prompting: Prompting is the situation, which arises when a pupil expresses his inability to answer some questions in the class or his answer is incomplete. The teacher can ask such questions, which prompt the pupils in solving the already asked questions.

(2) Seeking further Information: In class, when the pupils are unable to answer any question or answer partially, then in order to receive complete and correct answer, the teacher can ask such questions by accepting that the answer given is correct, but the pupil should reveal more. There can be alternate answer to the question asked such as elaborate the answer more. In this way, the teacher can seek maximum information from the pupils.

(3) Refocussing: Sometimes, the teacher may ask probing questions to concentrate the attention of the pupils. For the very same purpose, the teacher may ask same question from other pupil. This is known as 'Refocussing.'

(4) Redirection: If the teacher wants to introduce the pupils with various aspects of the problem in classroom then he can ask the same question after slight changes in the language. This technique is known as 'Redirection'.

(5) Critical Awareness: In order to develop the reasoning power of the pupils in class, the teacher can ask questions bearing 'Why', by getting motivate from such questions, pupils involve themselves in the process of reasoning. This is known as 'Critical Awareness' technique.

Table 4.1

Components	Rating scale
Prompting	1
Seeking further information	2
Refocussing	3
Redirection	4
Increasing critical awareness	5

✍ ✍ ✍

5 Lesson Planning Based on Microteaching

● ● ●

LESSON PLAN — 1

Subject: English	**Date:** ....
Topic: Use of Articles	**Duration:** 6 minutes
	Class: 6th

Teacher's Activity	Student's Activity	Component Rating Scale
(i) How many alphabets are there in English?	Twenty–six.	1, 2 and 3
(ii) Which letters are vowels?	a, e, i, o and u.	1, 2 and 3
(iii) What are the rest of the letters called?	Consonants.	1, 2 and 3
(iv) Very good, do you know about articles?	....	2 and 4
(v) Well, *a*, *an* and *the* are called articles. They come before nouns.	Students will listen carefully and note down in their notebooks.	4 and 5
(vi) There are two kinds of articles, i.e. Definite Articles and Indefinite Articles.	Students will listen carefully and note down in their notebooks.	3, 4 and 5

(vii) *A* or *An* are called the Indefinite Articles because these usually leave indefinite the person or thing spoken of; as, a politician; that is, anyone of the politicians.	Students will listen carefully and note down in their notebooks.	1, 3, 4 and 5
(viii) 'The' is called the Definite Article because it normally points out some particular persons or things; as, He saw the politician; meaning that particular politician he saw.	Students will listen carefully and note down in their notebooks.	1, 3, 4 and 5
(ix) The indefinite article is used before singular countable nouns, e.g. a table, an apple, a boy, an egg, etc.	Students will listen carefully and note down in their notebooks.	1, 3, 4 and 5
(x) The definite article is used before singular countable nouns, plural countable nouns and uncountable nouns, e.g. the book, the books, the doctor, the cops, the milk, etc.	Students will listen carefully and note down in their notebooks.	1, 3, 4 and 5

LESSON PLAN — 2

Subject: English	Date: _____
Topic: Infinitive	Duration: 6 minutes
	Class: 7th

Teacher's Activity	Student's Activity	Component Rating Scale
(i) What is a subject of the sentence?	The part names the person or thing we are speaking about.	1, 2 and 3
(ii) Good, what do you know about verb?	The word asserts something about a person or thing.	1, 2 and 3
(iii) Now, tell me about 'object'.	The word or group of words, functioning as a noun or a pronoun that is influenced by a verb or a preposition.	1, 2 and 3
(iv) Do you know about infinitives?	....	2 and 4
(v) Read these sentences: *Vikas wants to go.* *They tried to find faults within us.* The forms *to go* and *to find* are "infinitives".	Students will listen carefully and note down in their notebooks.	1, 3, 4 and 5
(vi) The infinitive is the base of a verb, often followed by 'to'.	Students will listen carefully and note down in their notebooks.	1, 3, 4 and 5
(vii) The infinitive may be used like a noun: *(a) As the Subject of a verb:* To reign is worth ambition. To find fault is easy. *(b) As the Object of a verb:* He likes to play cards. I do not mean to read.	Students will listen carefully and note down in their notebooks.	1, 3, 4 and 5

LESSON PLAN — 3

Subject: English	**Date:** _____
Topic: Participle	**Duration:** 6 minutes
	Class: 8th

Teacher's Activity	Student's Activity	Component Rating Scale
(i) What do you know about noun?	Words that used as the name of a person, place or thing.	1, 2 and 3
(ii) Good, what do you know about pronoun?	The words used instead of nouns.	1, 2 and 3
(iii) What do you know about adjectives?	Words that add before nouns.	1, 2 and 3
(iv) Good, do you know about participle?	....	2 and 4
(v) Read this sentence: *Hearing the noise, the boy woke up.* It is formed from the verb hear and governs an object.	Students will listen carefully and note down in their notebooks.	1, 3, 4 and 5
(vi) The word hearing, therefore, partakes of the nature of both verb and adjective, is called a participle.	Students will listen carefully and note down in their notebooks.	1, 3, 4 and 5
(vii) A participle is that form of verb, which partakes of the nature both of a verb and of an adjective.	Students will listen carefully and note down in their notebooks.	1, 3, 4 and 5
(viii) Study the following examples of participles: (a) The child, thinking all was safe, attempted to cross the road.	Students will listen carefully and note down in their notebooks.	1, 3, 4 and 5

(b)We met a boy carrying a basket of flowers. (c) Sohan rushed into the field and foremost fighting fell. The above are all examples of what is usually called the Present Participle, which ends with "ing" and represents an action as going on or incomplete or imperfect.		
(ix) Besides the present participle, we can form from each verb another participle called its past participle, which represents a completed action or state of the thing spoken of. The following are examples of past participles (a) Driven by hunger, they stole a piece of bread. (b) Children saw a few trees laden with fruits. (c) Deceived by his friend, Bhuvan lost all hope. It will be noticed that the past participle usually ends with –ed, –d, –en, –t, or –n.	Students will listen carefully and note down in their notebooks.	1, 3, 4 and 5

LESSON PLAN — 4

Subject: English	Date: _____
Topic: Gerund	Duration: 6 minutes
	Class: 9th

Teacher's Activity	Student's Activity	Component Rating Scale
(i) What do you know about nouns?	Words used as the name of a person, place or thing.	1, 2 and 3
(ii) What is a subject of the sentence?	The part names the person, or thing we are speaking about.	1, 2 and 3
(iii) Good, what do you know about verb?	Word that asserts something about a person or thing.	1, 2 and 3
(iv) Now, tell me about "object".	Words functioning as a noun or a pronoun, influenced by verb or preposition.	1, 2 and 3
(v) Do you know about gerund?	....	2 and 4
(vi) Read this sentence: *Singing is my favourite pastime.* The word singing is formed from the verb 'sing', by adding 'ing'. We also see that it is here used as the subject of a verb, and hence, does the work of a noun. It is therefore, a Verb–Noun and is called a Gerund.	Students will listen carefully and note down in their notebooks.	1, 3, 4 and 5

(vii) Some examples of Gerund are as follows: (a) I like reading G.P.H. books. (b) Playing cards is not allowed here. It will be noticed that the infinitive and the gerund are alike in being used as nouns, while still retaining the power that a verb has of governing another noun or pronoun in the objective case.	Students will listen carefully and note down in their notebooks.	1, 3, 4 and 5
(viii) Thus, a gerund is that form of verb, which ends with 'ing', and has the force of a noun and a verb.	Students will listen carefully and note down in their notebooks.	1, 3, 4 and 5
(ix) A gerund being a verb–noun may be used as: *(a) Subject of a verb:* Hunting animals is not allowed in this country. Seeing is believing. *(b) Object of a verb:* Stop talking. I am fond of swimming.	Students will listen carefully and note down in their notebooks.	1, 3, 4 and 5

✍ ✍ ✍

Wondering who is Gullybaba?

मुल्लीबाबा
Gullybaba

© Gullybaba is a combination of two significant words **'Gully'** & **'Baba'**. The word 'Gully' comes from the ancient game played in Rural India–**Tip cat.** In Hindi, we call it **Gully Danda** (गुल्ली डंडा) which is a great **symbol of Focus & Fitness.**

The word 'Baba' stands for **Respect & Honour.** And these are the fundamental parameters for achieving success. **Focus & Fitness** are required to help one go a long way in life. This is all about achieving excellence in education and giving respect & honour to everyone, and thus, the name 'Gullybaba'.

To know more about why name GullyBaba visit: **GullyBaba.com/why-name-gullybaba.html**

www.ingramcontent.com/pod-product-compliance
Lightning Source LLC
Chambersburg PA
CBHW071754090426
42737CB00012B/1818